Praise for *Love Imagined: a mixed race memoir*

Love Imagined: this fascinating, delightful, important book. This imagining love, this longing for love. This poverty of No Love, this persistent racism, sexism, classism, ageism. The pain these evils cause the soul. Sherry Lee "tiptoe[s] between a poverty of and a generosity of spirit," is a spirit of love that survives and infuses everything, even the doubts, fear and shame. This is an important document of a mixed-race contemporary woman, a memoir about her family lineages back to slavery, back to China, back to early Minneapolis, and about the struggle of finding herself in all of these. "Who am I? I'm the great-grandchild of Black female slaves and white men. I'm the great American Narrative." And she's the daughter of a man native to China. "I can easily say I am Black, just as I can easily say I am Asian... Rarely do I say I'm white, but genetically and culturally I am that too..." "I am each of these, yet all of these." "Racism and its dangers caused my mother to pass for white. I refuse to lie, but history has made it safer for me not to." Most simply I love reading this sassy, serious woman. Sherry Quan Lee is love imagined.

Sharon Doubiago, *Hard Country, The Book of Seeing with One's Own Eyes, Love on the Streets, My Father's Love*, etc.

To borrow a word from Toni Morrison, Sherry Quan Lee's beautiful and urgent book is an act of sovereignty. Transgressing through and disrupting multiple margins and in/visibilities, Quan Lee's words, especially the heart-breaking repetition of the word Shame, come searing through, page after page. This book is a voice in the wilderness. Quan Lee's bold, unapologetic, intimate, wise voice is an essential one.

Sun Yung Shin, author of *Rough, and Savage* and *Skirt Full of Black*.

In *Love Imagined* Sherry Quan Lee explores her family's mixed racial heritage and her own life with great courage and compelling honesty. She makes her deeply moving story our story as a country. She reveals her past as our past. This is an important and essential book.

David Mura, author of *Turning Japanese: Memoirs of a Sansei, Famous Suicides of the Japanese Empire, The Last Incantations*, etc.

Love Imagined is an important book because we, as Mixed-Race people (and the people who love us!) need to hear these stories. Because we are inherently not like the people from whom we came, it is vitally important that we connect and share our stories with one another. To be understood in an effortless way. When I read Sherry's story, I recognized feelings and meanings that mirrored mine. I felt a sense of release, an exhale, and I knew I could be understood by her in a way that some of my family and friends are unable to grasp, through no fault of their own. It's the Mixed experience. Sherry Lee's voice, her story, will no doubt touch and heal many who read it.

> Lola Osunkoya
> MA in Adlerian Counseling and Psychotherapy
> Founder of Neither/Both LLC
> Mixed-Race Community Building and Counseling

Joining the long history of women of color fighting to claim literary space to tell our stories, Sherry Quan Lee shares her truth with fierce courage and strength in *Love Imagined*. Weaving together the impact of geographic space, and a rich sense of temporal realities through her lens as a mixed-race, Chinese, Black woman, Quan Lee crafts a riveting tale of Minnesota life set within the backdrop of racial segregation, the Cold War, the sexual revolution while navigating it all through the lens of her multi-layered identities. A true demonstration of the power of an intersectional perspective, Quan Lee's memoir braids together the fragments of racialized, gendered, and sexual identities. In the spirit of the foremothers and those who will continue behind, through her poetic frame; a stirring tale that asks us to think about our assumptions and recognize the social constructs that shape and confine us all.

> Kandace Creel Falcón, Ph.D.
> Director of Women's and Gender Studies
> Minnesota State University Moorhead

LOVE IMAGINED:

a mixed race memoir

Sherry Quan Lee

Modern History Press

From the Reflections of America Series
2nd Printing - June 2015
Learn more at http://blog.sherryquanlee.com

Library of Congress Cataloging-in-Publication Data

Lee, Sherry Quan, 1948-
  Love imagined : a mixed race memoir / by Sherry Quan Lee.
    pages cm. -- (World voices)
  Includes bibliographical references and index.
  ISBN 978-1-61599-233-1 (pbk. : alk. paper) -- ISBN 978-1-61599-234-8
(hardcover : alk. paper) -- ISBN 978-1-61599-235-5 (ebook)
  1. Lee, Sherry Quan, 1948- 2. Poets, American--Biography. 3. Racially mixed
people--United States--Biography. I. Title.
  PS3562.E3644Z46 2014
  811'.54--dc23
  [B]
                                        2014011837

Modern History Press is an imprint of
Loving Healing Press
5145 Pontiac Trail
Ann Arbor, MI 48105
USA

Tollfree (USA/CAN): 888-761-6268
Fax: 734-663-6861

info@ModernHistoryPress.com
www.ModernHistoryPress.com

Distributed by Ingram Book Group (USA/CAN), Bertrams Books (UK/EU).

Along with the idea of romantic love, she was introduced to another—physical beauty. Probably the most destructive ideas in the history of human thought.

–*The Bluest Eye*, Toni Morrison

Dedicated to my cousin, Jay Sandvik

Contents

Disclaimer

Love Imagined is memoir. It is the truth of my life as I remember it; others may remember it differently, but this is my story, my identity—my life influenced by people and places and my own conscious and unconscious relationship to historical events.

Family members and others named in *Love Imagined* have chosen to read it or not; various individuals have given verbal permission to include stories that involve them and to use their names or not.

I have changed or used generic names as needed for privacy. Also, because I write under a last name different from any of my siblings or children or ex-husbands, privacy is respected as much as possible. Sister is often used generically to respect the identity of my three older sisters. I have only one brother.

Love Imagined is but a blip in a lifetime of skirmishes looking for love. Much has been deleted, much added, more deleted, more added. It is difficult to be succinct, to write memoir versus autobiography. Memoir is more than memory; it's memory unleashed, memory named, memory diagnosed, memory organized and reorganized—and brought to healthy conclusions.

I am a poet; this is my first attempt to write book-length prose; an attempt to reveal my story in depth, leaving less to metaphor, and to the imagination. Yet, to imagine is what my story strives to do, to see beyond what was and what is—not only to witness, but to attempt to decipher.

Foreword

In *Love Imagined*, Sherry Lee very openly and courageously tells her story. Yet only some of us will understand on a base level how courageous an act this is. In my personal experience as a Biracial woman, through my research, and in my experience working in the mental health field, I've come to understand how lonely and isolating an experience it can be to grow up as a Mixed-Race person. We are inherently not like our mother or father, and can have completely different phenotypes and experiences of race than our siblings. Depending on a number of factors—the attitudes about race of our family members and friends, our childhood and later life experiences, the types of racism and micro aggressions we experience, and how the people we care about react to us—the Mixed experience can fall anywhere on the range of positive to negative, and can include large portions of silent shame.

Sherry Lee does a beautiful job of bringing her experience to life. She paints a colorful, detailed, and poetic picture of her life that is brutally honest. She invites the reader in to experience how she made sense of her life, and the ways that shame began to permeate her sense of identity. Feelings of shame mixed with deep desire for love and acceptance mixed with a courageous, imaginative, persevering spirit are all intertwined in this beautiful story. A story that ultimately illustrates a road to self-acceptance.

Love Imagined is an important book because we, as Mixed-Race people (and the people who love us!) need to hear these stories. Because we are inherently not like the people from whom we came, it is vitally important that we connect and share our stories with one another. To be understood in an effortless way. When I read Sherry's story, I recognized feelings and meanings that mirrored mine. I felt a sense of release, an exhale, and I knew I could be understood by her in a way that some of my family and friends are unable to grasp, through no fault of their own. It's the Mixed experience. Sherry Lee's voice, her story, will no doubt touch and heal many who read it.

Lola Osunkoya
MA in Adlerian Counseling and Psychotherapy
Founder of Neither/Both LLC
Mixed-Race Community Building and Counseling

Introduction

> Who am I? Who do I think I am? Am I the only real liar in my family? Am I the only one who didn't understand my mother's warning, "don't go near the water, you might drown"? Am I merely the white girl I was culturally raised to be?

Love Imagined is a glimpse into my life. It is my story, not the story of my mother, my father, my siblings, or of relatives known or unknown. However my story makes mention of stories that belong to others where needed because lives and history intersect.

My story is unique, just as your story is unique. Even though we may have DNA alike or similar to someone else, many factors affect who we are such as who we know, where we live, our education, our politics, our religion, whether we have children or not, what age we are, our gender, our sexuality, and what color our skin is.

Thus, as your read *Love Imagined* be prepared to set aside your prejudices. Be prepared to understand that memoir is not myth, but truth. If you think, as you read, I am a "tragic mulatto," know that I am not. My life is not tragic. Traumatic at times certainly, but well-lived, and no regrets.

"Tragic mulatto" is a literary myth that goes back to slavery times. It refers to mixed-race Black and white people, especially women, who are unable to fit into society because whites don't want them and Blacks don't want them-- nobody wants them--but, truly, they were desired, and often raped. According to myth, many became despondent and some attempted suicide.

Mulatto is a derogatory term. I am not mulatto (I am not a mule, not the child of a horse and a donkey). I detest labels, yet sometimes we are forced to self-identify. I have used biracial, mixed-race, African American, Black, Chinese, Chinese and Black, and Other; as well as lesbian, bisexual—fem; as well as mother, wife, divorced, single; as well as mother-in-law, and grandmother; as well as writer, teacher, mentor. My identity is a wealth of adjectives and nouns claiming who I am.

Yes, it's true, I have been rejected by suitors because of their parents' prejudices, and or their own—or I've rejected them. And, yes, I have been despondent. And, yes, I have attempted suicide. However, I am more than myth. I have never kept my identity a secret, except when my mother told me I had to, and that was before I even understood what my identity was. I have challenged myth by acting and reacting, by writing and speaking. However, I am not fiction, perhaps not even literature. Perhaps I am not even a *writer*. But, I have a story to tell. And, when the suffering is unbearable, and I do suffer (who doesn't), I have many options and allies to help me get through it. The truth is I am still alive.

Whites like me, Asians like me, Blacks like me; I am each of these, yet all of these. I can easily say I am Black, just as I can easily say I am Asian without having to say I am Black and Asian, because I am. Rarely do I say I'm white, but genetically and culturally I am that too. But the construct of race and the *one-drop rule* relegated me to Black, even though one could argue that my father is more Chinese than my mother is Black, and if there weren't that one-drop rule, that would be true.

Racism and its dangers caused my mother to pass for white. I refuse to lie, but recent history has made it safer for me not to.

Acknowledgements

A lifetime of thanks to the many people who have contributed, or will contribute, to my understanding of who I am, some whom I've never met including authors and singers who have influenced me. Some of you have come in and out of my life so quickly, a whisper, a gentle breeze; others have been faithful friends for decades. You are all remembered and appreciated. Thank you for contributing to my survival.

Thank you Victor R. Volkman, publisher, for continuing to have faith in me, even as I ventured into prose. Sharon Doubiago, editor, your enthusiasm for *Love Imagined* from its infancy, and throughout its growth pains, has been a blessing; thank you so much. I especially appreciate that you believed in my story, my American narrative, and insisted I keep writing.

Thanks to Sun Yung Shin and Lori Young-Williams for taking the time out of your busy professional and personal lives to read and comment on *Love Imagined*. Charissa Uemura, thanks for supporting me over the years; thank you for taking photos of me and reformatting photographs from my past—and thanks for sharing stories and cinnamon rolls over the years. Patricia Holter Ronken, how you surprised me; thank you for volunteering to do a final copy edit the day the final manuscript was due, but most of all thank you for remembering stories from our childhood that I didn't remember.

Thank you Jay Sandvik (my cousin, my mother's sister's son), your insistence that I write my story, even though or maybe because it intersects with your story, has kept me writing, especially in times of my most agonizing uncertainty. Thank you for taking the time to read and comment on several drafts of *Love Imagined* over the years, and filling in blanks about our mothers' family.

And to my cousin's daughter, I will be ever grateful for your encouraging words that have given me reason to keep on writing over the years despite my anxiety and fears:

July 16, 1993

Sherry,

It is 9:30pm on a Friday night, I've just returned from the laundry room where my favorite "blankee" is happily washing. I settled into a comfortable spot to read your article, A Little Mixed Up, published in the July/August issue of "colors".

As I write, I shed tears of joy and pain. Reading the thoughts and notes of my patrilineal family members, forced the realization of excruciating loss and triumphant gains.

Until this moment, I never realized what I lost when my grandmother died. The note dated February 17th, 1948, in your article, could have been written by my own hand. These are _my_ thoughts and deepest "Knowings" today! The same thoughts, unbeknowst to me until now, my own grandmother penned, 45 years ago. I feel great sadness that we, my grandmother and I, were unable to share our thoughts with each other, a 'missed opportunity' within our battle scarred family.

Sherry, I thank you from the core of my being. I thank you for being, for your courageous writings, the gift, to our entire family, of your (our) innermost thoughts of pride and pain. I thankyou for 'thinking for yourself' and I thank you for gracefully dealing the blows of "multi-cultural" reality, through your conscious efforts to enlighten the fearful, of this racist, ethnocentric world,

Country, state, city. I thank you for
opening an intimate connection for
me to my past and future.

truly yours,
Terri
thankyou

I also extend thanks to my siblings and my sons who may have had concerns about the personal nature of *Love Imagined*, but didn't ask me to stop writing. I tried to keep my story my story, but you are family, there's no denying it.

Thank you Mother for all you gave and gave up. The tough choices you made to keep your children safe.

Aunt Grace, thank you for the legacy you left me of your words in poetry and prose. Father, thank you for your legacy, your handwritten journal given to me a few months before you died. Without the written work of family, my story would be greatly left to imagination, as is love.

South Scandinavian Minneapolis

The bones of Chinese girls' feet, as young as two years old, were broken and bound in lengths of cloth to stop their growth. Three-inch feet were deemed sexy, thus poor women with lotus feet could possibly marry into a wealthy family.

The practice of footbinding ended in 1949 (although it had been outlawed as early as 1912), the year the People's Republic of China was founded by Mao Zedong, Chairman of the Communist Party of China—*I was one year old*.

Once upon a very long time ago there was a princess, Quan Lee, born 1948. She was no ordinary princess. Her kingdom was a house on a hill with a white picket fence in South Scandinavian Minneapolis. She lived in a world of make believe.

> I am dressed in Chinese silk pajamas with tiny frog closures. The Mandarin collar is choking my smile. I am looking away from the camera. Down the street. Past the Lutheran church. Past the homes of the little blonde girls who attend the Lutheran church Sunday school with me. Past the family I don't know. The family that does not recognize me. My family.

> *–Black White Chinese Women Got the Beat*,
> performance by Sherry Quan Lee and Lori Young-Williams

She was Cinderella awaiting her prince. She loved her shoes. She sang to them. Hugged them. Loved them. Loved every pair of fake Capezio flats her dollar a week allowance allowed her to buy. Maybe it was the black patent leather shoes her mother, raising her on welfare, managed to buy for her every Easter that began her obsession for pretty footwear. Maybe she knew that beauty was bound in binding a young girl's feet, that somehow history had whispered to her *it's always about finding the prince*, no matter how painful the journey, no matter how many pairs of shoes it would take.

Recently my friend Carolyn challenged me about my use of the term *South Scandinavian Minneapolis*, where I grew up. As a writer, I know it's important to be specific. Specifically, I grew up in a house on a hill on 26th Avenue and 39th Street, two blocks west of Roosevelt High School, the Roosevelt Public Library, Our Redeemer Lutheran Church, The Ritz Grocery Store, and Herman's grocery store.

East of Roosevelt High School, on Hiawatha Avenue, was Beek's, "the king of pizza." South of Roosevelt High School was Scott's Pharmacy. A couple blocks farther south is Lake Hiawatha Park.

North and west of where I lived was Folwell Junior High School. My sister, various neighborhood friends, and I walked the mile to school every day even in frigid Minnesota weather. On the way home from school we would pass the Nile Theater on 23rd Avenue, then walk down 38th Street where we sometimes stopped at the soda fountain in the Nile Pharmacy, or stopped at Little Tony's Italian Restaurant for french fries and a cherry coke. Sometimes we ran past the shoe shop to Harper's Variety Store on the corner to buy trading cards.

Five blocks west of where I lived was Miles Standish Elementary School. We walked to school, home for lunch, back to school, and home again. Two blocks west of Standish is Sibley Park where, in junior high school, we went to the Friday night dances (my sister was Sibley Park Snow Queen one year; I was never a queen, only a wallflower).

According to the City of Minneapolis I lived in the Standish Neighborhood:

The Standish neighborhood on Minneapolis' south side, is bound on the north by 36th Street, on the east by Hiawatha Avenue, on the south by 42nd and 43rd streets and on the west by Cedar Avenue. This neighborhood was named after an area elementary school, which had been called Miles Standish after a work by the poet Henry Wadsworth Longfellow. The area was considered the outskirts of the city until immigrants, mostly Swedish and Norwegian, began building their homes here early in the 1900s.

My grandparents and my mother and her siblings grew up east of where I grew up, bordering the Longfellow neighborhood on 25th Street, near Snelling Avenue (not the Snelling Avenue in St. Paul). From what I know they attended Longfellow grade school. The railroads in the area provided employment for Black men; Grandpa was a porter for one of the railroad lines running into Chicago.

Aunt Grace wrote: "We did not live in a Black ghetto. Our home was the lower left apartment on East 25th Street. It was rented, at that time, to colored tenants only." She also wrote that her mama and papa were "highly respected by [their] white neighbors. The only trouble that I can remember, we had at the hands of the Black people in the tenement." This was because a neighbor had told their friends they were "passing for white." They weren't. But later, my mother and her children living in South Scandinavian Minneapolis, were.

My friend, Carolyn, was right. Carolyn, a Black woman, lived in South Minneapolis too. She went to Central High School. My cousin, both parents Black, went to Central High School. Carolyn had a crush on my cousin. (Other cousins went to North High School.)

My friend, Carolyn, my Aunt Marion (my mother's youngest sister) and her son (my cousin), lived in South Minneapolis, but they lived with Black folk, unlike me who lived east of whatever line divided us.

I didn't know much about geography when I was little, but I did know my mother's family could only visit at night, when it was dark, and our neighbors couldn't see them.

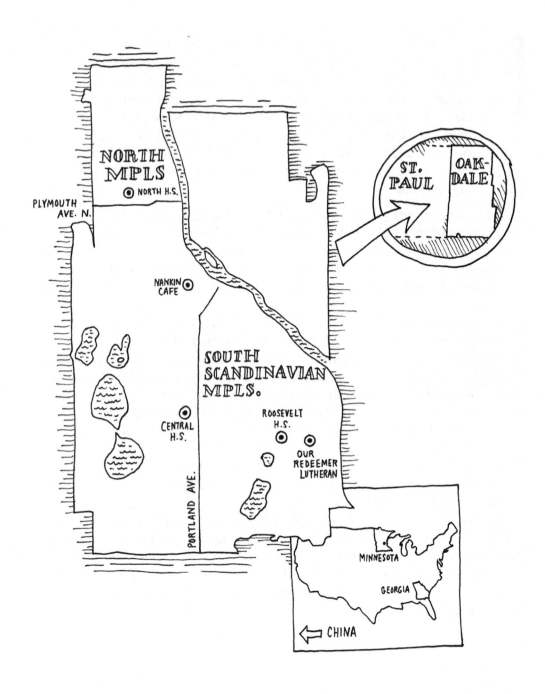

MPLS Area Map by Andy Sturdevant

North Minneapolis

Aunt Grace, third in line of the Franklin sisters (my mother was second in line), lived in North Minneapolis in a Duplex on Emerson Avenue North. This is where Grandma, my mother's mom, also lived, perhaps after Grandpa died, I'm not sure. It must have been sometime after Grandma died of self-inflicted poisoning, when the cancer was more painful than she could bear, that my Aunt Grace and her family moved farther west, trespassing into the Jewish neighborhood, 16th and Vincent Avenue North between West Broadway Avenue and Plymouth Avenue North. Streets and Avenues don't change, but people coming and going do.

I remember we visited Aunt Grace, my mom, my sisters and I. We took a bus down Broadway, stopped to shop at thrift stores, and then walked to the most beautiful home I had ever seen.

Another aunt and her children lived for a time in one of the north side housing projects off Olson Memorial Highway (Sumner Field, Glenwood, Lyndale and Olson public housing developments). Since then, the projects have been torn down, and in 2005-2009 the modern Heritage Park Community which includes a park, apartments, for-sale homes, and a senior center was created, due to a law suit claiming segregation in public housing.

When I turned nineteen, I brought my childhood friend, Annie, to visit my Aunt Grace in North Minneapolis. Annie remembers my mother being quite angry with me. But Annie knew, despite my mother's passing jones, that I was Black. She said everyone in the neighborhood knew. Everyone except me.

Despite my mother's angst, I wanted to know her family. So over the years I continued to integrate myself into the Black family I had been segregated from for too many years.

After my mom and dad divorced, my dad eventually moved with his new Bohemian wife and Chinese/Bohemian children to the Camden area, upper north side of Minneapolis, near the Weber Park swimming pool, where my mother's sister's son lived close enough to walk to school with my father's children.

In the 1980s I participated in writing workshops, and taught a writing workshop in North Minneapolis at the Pillsbury Oak Park Community Center. My first public poetry reading was at a North Side coffee house.

Flashback: when I was in high school, 1963-1966, Mother didn't allow me to go to Roosevelt vs. North football games played at North High School. She said there might be a race riot. I didn't know what she was talking about.

The Personal is Political

I am sixty-three years old. I wear white tennis shoes, black leather flats, red cowboy boots, and pink high heels. Pairs of recycled Stuart Weitzman, Joan and David, Marc Fisher, Nine West, and Steve Madden shoes line the shelves of my bedroom closet. Each pair calling me to attention. Each pair soliciting happily ever after. Shoes, the sensuous, seductive icons of the twenty-first century.

No man gets to glimpse my menagerie of seduction. No man is allowed in my bedroom, or my writing room—not any more, or at least not today.

My hopes and dreams, yes, I still have them, are no longer an open book, but a little girl's diary locked until someone appears with the only key.

However, today I am reminiscing; I am writing. I am allowing myself to be vulnerable. I am imagining what has been locked away for so many years. Locked away like my Black relatives who could only visit the house on the hill in South Minneapolis at night when the neighbors couldn't distinguish them as anything more than shadows, as secrets climbing the red brick stairs and entering the stucco house, lights off, blinds closed.

I am imagining my Chinese father who, unlike my Black relatives, slithered out the door instead of in, disappearing in the night as if again taking on another identity as he did when he left China, a young boy slipping into a foreign culture, the USA, to earn money to send home to his mother because his father died and he, being the eldest child, was responsible for his family's welfare.

It is not easy to write my story. For years I wrote my story in fragments of not so poetic lines. I spit out anger and revenge, sharp knives cutting through every other line with just enough sass to bear my wounds. I couldn't stop incriminating just about everyone and every institution—schools, churches, places of business, etc., calling out injustices with every harsh word, hoping my poems would birth me, and make sense of who I was and why I wasn't happy.

There are moments I am still not happy. The absence of love debilitating. The need, not only to be loved, but to love someone. The fear of being alone. Being alone. Poverty of the spirit. Poverty.

Maybe it was the chokecherry tree in my childhood backyard that is the metaphor for my writing life. Ripe berries seducing birds to eat, then shit white; droppings scattered like my poems. A professor, reading between my lines, asked if magnolias in my poem "Wintergreen" represented Black men lynched, or if the chokecherry tree in my poem "Chokecherry" signified the tree on Sethe's back (*Color Purple* by Alice Walker). She assumed they were conscious choices. They weren't.

Wintergreen

Minnesota is not compatible
to my growth, it is too cold.

The Ice Age made it clear
Magnolias, you can live
here in SE China, here in Georgia.

My ancestors oppose the heat.

Civil wars and death or just a robin
traveling against the season—
tossed Black /tossed Chinese:

Here I am, a Minnesota mutant.
Snowflake.

Like a magnolia, I am
not white. It is only light
passing through. Mama
cooked tuna noodle casserole
and daddy ate it.

Like a magnolia
—whose sepals never fuse—
my life is disparate
                here a Black
                community,
        there an Asian
        community,
                everywhere, white.

Sherry Quan Lee, *Chinese Blackbird*

Memory resides in the body, in the mind, and appears when I'm not looking. I believe my physical body and the body of my poems unconsciously uncover a history I didn't know.

I believe the personal *IS* political, as many before me have claimed. I believe that a mixed-race child passing for white, growing up in the sixties was more than bell bottom jeans and psychedelic music. That the freedom my peers sought was different from the freedom I ached for. I wanted what they had, the *Ozzie and Harriet* life. They ran from it, I ran toward it. I ran towards love.

Write About Your Chinese Father

In 1940 there were not enough Asian and Pacific Islanders in Minnesota to count as a percentage; in 1950 0.1% were APIs. 2012 data shows Asians as 4.4% of Minnesota's population (this does not include Asians who reported being of more than one race).

–U.S. Census Bureau[1]

Write about your Chinese father, a friend said to me. *Write about your Chinese father, your Chinese father, your Chinese…*what I heard: *Asians are in, Asians are exotic, Asians are a commodity.*

It wasn't that I wasn't interested in knowing my father, even though he left my mother (when I was five years old), or my mother kicked him out (who to believe) because he came home, again, in the wee hours of a Sunday morning as neighbors headed for church. Knowing my father wasn't a priority because I was allowed to be Chinese, if necessary, if the neighborhood kids didn't believe I was white. I was allowed to eat chow mein and play Mahjong. Black was a secret; Chinese was, when necessary, just an *exotic* admission.

My father had many names. His obituary reads "William (Theun) Wing, age 85, born March 3, 1909 in Canton, China." *The Manifest of Alien Passengers on the S.S. China* dated November 22, 1919 records my father's name as "Quan, Wing

---

[1] http://quickfacts.census.gov/qfd/states/27000.html

Theun." His senior class yearbook records his last name as Billy Quon.

I know him as Billy Quan. His "life story" as told by him with handwritten stories, photocopies of his family in China and a few relatives in the United States, and documents from World War II, that he gave to me a few months before he died, is how I know him; yet, mostly what I know of him is the absence of him. (Stories from my father's journal have been transcribed precisely as he wrote them, honoring that English was his second language. I do not know how old my father was when he wrote this journal.)

MY FIRST TEN YEARS OF MY LIFE WAS SPEND IN CHINA IN THE VILLAGE OF HAI PING. I WAS TOO YOUNG TO REMEMBER TOO MUCH. THE VILLAGE WAS CONSIST OF ROW OF HOUSE—EIGHT TO TEN IN A ROW RUN NORTH TO SOUTH. THERE WERE ABOUT TEN ROW. AT THE HEAD OF THE VILLAGE WAS A SCHOOL HOUSE. MY GRANDFATHER WAS THE PROFESSOR. ...

MY FATHER PASSED AWAY WHEN I WAS SEVEN. WHEN MY UNCLE (HO) WAS HOME FROM UNITED STATES TO VISIT HIS FAMILY THEY DECIDED TO HAVE ME JOIN HIM WHEN HE RETURN TO THE STATE, I BEING THE OLDEST WAS THE HEAD OF FAMILY HAVE TO MAKE MONEY TO SUPORT THE FAMILY. I WAS ONLY TEN AT THE TIME. WHEN WE LEFT FOR U.S.A. I LEFT MY MOTHER AND YOUNGER BROTHER AND SISTER. NEVER TO SEE THEM AGAIN. THE TRIP FROM THE VILLAGE TO HONG KWONG— WAS ONE DAY. WHERE WE BOARD THE STEAM SHIP S.S. CHINA. IT TOOK US TWO WEEKS TO REACH THE STATES BY THE WAY OF HONOLULO AND SAN FRANCISCO.

WE STAY IN SAN FRANCISCO ABOUT A MONTH AND THEN WE HEADED FOR LOS ANGELES WHERE MY UNCLE HAD A JOB WAITING FOR HIM. HE WAS A COOK AND A VERY GOOD ONE. WHILE IN LOS ANGELES I STAYED AT MY RELATIVE WHO OWN A CHINESE HERB STORE. MY UNCLE'S JOB WAS AT A SMALL TOWN FROM L.A. HE WAS ALWAYS WORKING—SO I NEVER GET TO SEE HIM TOO MUCH. I WAS AT MY OWN FOR A ELEVEN YEARS BOY. I LEARN MY ENGLISH AT A SMALL MISSIONARY SCHOOL. THE ONLY TIME I HAD TROUBLE-WITH UNCLE-WAS I WENT TO A MOVIE AND STAY AND SAW THE MOVIE THREE TIMES. IT WAS A COWGIRL PICTURE.

MY FATHER PASSED AWAY WHEN I WAS SEVEN, WHEN
MY UNCLE (HO) WAS HOME FROM UNITED STATES TO
VISIT HIS FAMILY THEY DECIDED TO HAVE ME JOIN
HIM WHEN HE RETURN TO THE STATE, I BEING THE OLDEST
WAS THE HEAD OF FAMILY HAVE TO MAKE MONEY TO
SUPORT THE FAMILY. I WAS ONLY TEN AT THE TIME
WHEN WE LEFT FOR U.S.A I LEFT MY MOTHER AND
YOUNGER BROTHER AND SISTER. NEVER TO SEE THEM
AGAIN. THE TRIP FROM THE VILLAGE TO HONG KWONG
WAS ONE DAY. WHERE WE BOARD THE STEAM SHIP S.S.
CHINA. IT TOOK US TWO WEEKS TO REACH THE STATES
BY THE WAY OF HONOLULO AND SAN FRANSISCO, WE
STAY IN SAN FRANCISCO ABOUT A MONTH. AND THEN
WE HEADED FOR LOS ANGELES WHERE MY UNCLE
HAD A JOB WAITING FOR HIM. HE WAS A COOK
AND A VERY GOOD ONE. WHILE IN LOS ANGELES I
STAYED AT MY RELATIVE WHO OWN A CHINESE
HERB STORE. MY UNCLE'S JOB WAS AT A SMALL
TOWN FROM L.A. HE WAS ALWAY WORKING SO
I NEVER GET TO SEE HIM TOO MUCH. I WAS AT
MY OWN FOR A ELEVEN YEARS BOY. I LEARN
MY ENGLISH AT A SMALL MISSARY SCHOOL.
THE ONLY TIME I HAD TROUBLE WITH UNCLE
WAS I WENT TO A MOVIE AND STAY AND SAW
THE MOVIE THREE TIMES. IT WAS A COW-
GIRL PICTURE.

My dad graduated from Santa Anna High School in 1932, where he was on the yearbook staff, and was on the football team, basketball team, baseball team, track team, and wrestling team. (He never got to know my sons, so he never knew they too were athletes. They ran track and cross country, played hockey, played tennis, and one son is now an avid baseball player.)

But after a year of attending Santa Anna Junior College, my father, along with a friend who was visiting his aunt in Santa Anna, rode the rails to Chicago to see the World's Fair. My dad said he was worried because there were bums all over the place and he was the only one with money. When he got to Chicago his friend took off.

Dad got a job as a dishwasher for a ladies' cafeteria. His salary was $5.50 a week and he worked from 5:00 AM until 6:00 PM. After three or four months he got a job at the Stanley Café making $6.50 per week. He could buy a meal for ten cents and he could see two features at the burlesque show for ten cents!

In Chicago Dad met the Kim Loo Sisters who were playing at the State and Lake Theatre. They were from Minneapolis. Their father is Chinese, their mother Polish. My father moved to Minneapolis in 1933 when the Kim Loo sisters' father invited him to chauffeur the sisters to their dance events. For five years he chauffeured the Kim Loo sisters while working part-time at the Nankin Café as a busboy. The Kim Loo sisters' father worked at the Nankin as a waiter and he got my father the job:

> The Nankin Café, which opened in its first location in Minneapolis in 1919, was for many years the center of Minnesota Chinese cultural life. In 1948, Nankin owner and Chef Walter James—with the help of his friend Stanley Chong—converted part of the Café into clubrooms for the growing Chinese community. James and Chong founded the organization that eventually became the Chinese American Association of Minnesota (CAAM). [2]

> At a time when Chinese-American entertainers were a rarity, the Kim Loo Sisters shared top billing with such stars as Frank Sinatra, Jackie Gleason and Ann Miller. And though the prevalent media stereotype of Chinese women was either Dragon Lady (femme fatale), Suzie Wong (sexual plaything) or Madame Butterfly (submissive spouse/dutiful daughter), the four sisters personified not one but two all-American icons of the 40s—the girl next door and the pinup girl, albeit and improbably in Chinese dress. (Leslie Li)[3]

---

[2] http://www.mnhs.org/events/ChineseAmerican/exhibit5.html
[3] http://www.leslieli.com/ldl/about.html

My father met my mother, a Black woman handing out towels to white ladies in the bathroom, at the Nankin Café. *Shame.* They married in 1937 and lived downtown, on Glenwood and Seventh, across from what is now the First Avenue nightclub, a short walk from the Nankin.

I didn't know when I was growing up, what I know now, that if my mother and father had lived in almost any state other than Minnesota (one of eight states that never passed anti-miscegenation laws) they couldn't have legally married.

Their first child was born in 1941, the second in 1943. Married with two children, my father joined the Navy to serve in World War II. He was discharged December 1945.

THEN I SIGN UP FOR SERVICE IN THE NAVY. AT GREAT LAKE I TOOK SOME I.Q. TEST AND PASS FOR A RADIO MAN. THE NAVY SEND ME TO NORTH-WESTERN COLLEGE IN RADIO. I WAS THERE FOR ONE YEAR AND I HAD A BALL ALL THE TIME. EVERY WEEK END I WOULD GO TO CHICAGO WENT TO U.S.O. AND GET TICKETS FOR MOVIE AND BALL GAMES. FREE MEALS AND FREE RIDES HOME. I PLAYED ON OUR SOFTBALL TEAM. I WAS THE PITCHER. WE HAD A GOOD TEAM. I ALSO WON SECOND PLACE IN THE SCHOOL DECA-THLON EVENT. AFTER SCHOOL I WAS SENT TO SAN DIEGO FOR MY ASSIGEMENT. MY FRIEND MABEL AND KENNY WAS LIVING THERE. WE HAD WORK TOGETHER AT THE NANKIN. KENNY USED TO TRAIN MARINE. THEY TOLD ME THE OFFICER CLUB NEEDED A BARTENER. I APPLIED FOR THE JOB AND GOT IT. I WORK THERE FOR ABOUT THREE WEEKS. THEY PAID ME FIVE DOLLARS A DAY WHEN I WAS SUPPOSE TO GET THREE DOLLARS. WHILE THERE A GROUP OF SHOW PEOPLE WAS PLAYING. THEY WERE BING CROBY, BOB HOPE, FRANCIS LANGFORD AND JERRY COLONE. WHEN THEY LEFT THEY PASS BY MY STATION AND BOB HOPE STOP AND SPEAK TO ME. I FINALLY GET MY SHIP ASSIGMENT TO LST 951.

MY BOSS AT THE NAVY CLUB TOLD ME HE TRY TO HAVE ME STAY AT THE CLUB. HE COULDN'T BECAUSE I BELONG TO A SPECIAL GROUP. THEY GAVE ME TEN DOLLAR AND A BOTTLE OF SCOTCH

FOR XMAS. WHEN I GOT ABOARD THE LST 951 WE HEADED FOR PEARL HARBOR. AFTER WE ARRIVED THERE OUR SHIP WAS ASSIGNED LST 951 (H) A CASUALTY EVACUATION CONTROL SHIP.

LST 951 Photo posted by Jeffrey McDonald

WE CARRY MANY DOCTOR AND MEDICAL SUPPLIES ON BOARD. WHILE IN PEARL HARBOR I SAW ALL OUR SHIPS SINK INTO THE BAY, TERRIBLE SIGHTS. AFTER A WEEK IN PEARL HARBOR WE JOIN WITH GROUP OF OTHER SHIPS TO MANDOVER FOR THE INVASION OF OKINAWO. IT WAS THE BIGGEST FLOATATION OF SHIPS PUT TOGETHER. OVER 1,000 SHIPS. THE INVASION WAS ON SUNDAY 9 AM IN THE MORNING APRIL FOOL DAY. OUR SHIP WAS AMONG THE FIRST GROUP. THERE WERE LOTS OF ACTION, BUT I DIDN'T GET INTO ANY PART OF THE ACTION, BECAUSE BEING A RADIO MAN JUST WAS SUPPOSE TO STAY IN THE RADIO ROOM. I COULD ONLY PEEK THRU THE KEYHOLE. HEARD OF BOOMING-OF BIG GUNS- AND LOTS OF PLANES OVERHEAD. AT NITE I USE TO GO UP DECK AND WATCH THE BATTLESHIP FIRING THEIR FLAMING BULLLITS TOWARD THEIR MARK AND THEN BURSTING INTO FLAMES AS THEY HIT. LIGHTING THE SKY FOR OUR GROUND CREWS.

IN DECEMBER, 1945 I WAS READY TO BE DISCHARGE INSTEAD OF BEING TO DISCHARGE IN MINNEAPOLIS I REQUEST TO BE DISCHARGE IN CALIFORNIA BECAUSE I WANTED TO SEE MY UNCLE. I HAD MY DISCHARGE MONEY $300 WITH ME AND I WANTED HIM TO SEND IT TO MY MOTHER IN CHINA. THE NAVY ALLOWED ME 5 CENTS PER MILE BACK TO MINNEAPOLIS SO I BOUGHT MY BUS FARE BACK TO MINNEAPOLIS. I HAD TO CHANGE BUS IN DES MOINES, IOWA, BUT I COULDN'T FIND MY OTHER HALF OF TICKET. I HAD TO BUY ANOTHER TICKET.

I ARRIVE HOME IN TIME TO CLEBRATE NEW YEAR EVE. JANUARY WALTER JAME PUT ME BACK TO WORK AS NITE MANGER. ALSO WHILE I WAS IN CALIFORNIA MY UNCLE TOLD ME MY COUSINS JEAN AND JOE WAS LIVING IN PHOENIX ARIZONA. I VIST THEM AND THEY TOLD ME MY SISTER GET MARRIED AND MOVED TO SINGAPORE. SHE PASSED AWAY DURING THE JAPANESE WAR. MY BROTHER REMAIN IN CHINA TO CARE FOR MY MOTHER.

Before Dad went to Chicago for Navy school, he was told married men were no longer needed, but he had already left his job and packed his bags. A letter he sent home to my mom while in the Navy:

When I get home we will run the house differently. I will write you a check for all bills and, etc. every month.

I'll see that you will always have money and I'll start a bank account for your own use of $100.00. That I hope will keep you in cigarettes. You will have at least two new dresses a year (on me). Of course I'll have a bank account too. Do I sound changed? I believe so! We will go out at least one nite a week (just us) and we will take the kids out one nite a week also (put this on your calendar).

A letter my mother sent to my father, November 5, 1945 starts:

Dear Billy, I had a letter from you Friday and one Saturday written when you were nearing Japan. ...Billy, it's so lonesome now that it's cold weather and we have to stay in all day. Hurry home to us.

–Your Three Sweethearts.

Nov. 5, 1945

Dear Billy:

I had a letter from you Friday and one Saturday, written when you were nearing Japan. I suppose by now you are back in Leyte.

I felt terrible when you said you wouldn't be back until January. I've been praying you would get back before Christmas.

Yesterday after Sunday School I took Sallie & Sue downtown to the show. Marion & Butch & Denny met us. We all went to the Pantages & saw "Up In Mabel's Room." It was very funny. After the

show we walked around
and let the kids look in
the windows. Then we
took them in Bridgmans
& all had a sundae.
I got home just in time
to listen to the Thin Man
and the other Sunday nite
programs.

Billy, its so lonesome
now that its cold weather
and we have to stay in
all day. Hurry home
to us.

Your three Sweethearts
Sarah, Sallie, Sue

nov.

rent	22.49
gas	1.50
elec	3.00
tel	3.16
oil	13.60
food	36.00
Wards	5.00
laundry	3.00
dancing lessons	4.00
2 pr. pants	1.00
1 slip	2.00
	94.75

shaw, carfare etc.   2.00
With the other 3.00 I
paid mama for keeping the
Kids while I went to cash
my check, and bought some
tooth powder, shoulder pads
snaps, and some stuff for
the Kids in the dime store.

Eighteen years and four going on five kids after they were married, my mom and dad divorced.

In 1976, at the age of 67, my dad retired from the Nankin Café. He told me he retired not because he had money, but because he was tired.

How difficult was it for my father, a man who liked to play like a boy, but was financially responsible for a family he pretended didn't exist, a new family, and a mother in China?

In 1993 I had a chance to go to Taiwan as a staff person for an independent study program (with a side trip to Hong Kong). Not knowing if I'd ever have the opportunity to travel to China, my father's birthplace, I sent a letter to my father along with an essay that I wrote about my trip.

I met a man in Taiwan, resident of Hong, who once hitchhiked in the United States. He said that he was given a ride by a man who took a liking to him. The man said if he ever needed anything he should go to a particular Chinese restaurant in Minneapolis, the Nankin, and ask for Harry Lee. He never did. I told him Harry Lee was the man I was named after. My father expected me, the fourth child, to be the boy he'd been waiting for. Harry Lee was the manager at the Nankin where my father worked.

My father's response to my letter was a letter to me, written on *USS LST 951 50*[th] *year reunion* stationery, 1994:

> Sherry: Enjoy reading your notes except where you wrote that I left your mother for another woman that's totally wrong. Your mother drove me out of the house. I didn't remarry for another two years. [He may not have remarried for two years but meanwhile my brother was born and a half-brother was born about the same time; my father finally got his son(s).]

I had heard this and that about the other woman after dad disappeared, perhaps from Mom talking to the neighbor lady. I remember going with them to a restaurant that I think my dad had bought (a detour, perhaps, from the Nankin, that didn't last long), to get a close look at the woman with red hair that my father eventually married.

I never questioned my mother's side of the story. I had no interest in my father. I didn't hate him or dislike him. I didn't know him, and I was okay with it (although now I wonder how much not having a father in a household of five women, affected my ability to have a stable relationship with any man, for better or worse). But now, I had my father's story, and what to do with it?

> I'm glad you had all that trip to the Orient. I wanted to see the Great Wall of China. I won't now. My health is just so, so. I am a diabetic for many years been on dialysis for four years now. I'm now 85 years old. The good Lord been good to me.

> I'm send you some things to read and some family pictures. Hope you enjoy them. I don't write too much and not often because my mind wanders off all the time and sometime I get stump on some small word.

> Enjoy your life fully—

> Dad

Boston, Mass.
LST 951 1994

USS LST 951

50th Year

Sherry:

Enjoy reading your notes. Except where you wrote that I left Your mother for another woman that's totally wrong. Your mother drove me out of house. I didn't remarry for another two years, you know I bought a good house for the family, build a big play house for your kid. Take the family on many trip. You know what she told every one that the trip was only for me. I bought new windows for the house and she said it for me. What broke my back was some furniture store send me a bill for things I

Boston, Mass.
LST 951 1 9 9 4

USS LST 951

I'm glad you had all that year(?) trip to the orient. I wanted to see the Great Walls of China. I won't now. my health is just so, so. I am a diabetic for many years been on dialysis(?) for four years now. I'm now 88 years old. The good lord been good to me.

I'm send you some things to read and some family pictures. hope you enjoy them. I don't write too much and not often. because my minds wonder off all the time and some time I get stump on some small word. Enjoy your life fully —

Dad

3

Dad did say *he was never late on all the support money*. And that was true. But, although he fought for visiting rights, I seldom saw him except when he drove down our alley, honked his horn, and one of us would run out to get the $7.00 per week per child support check from him. I remember one Christmas Eve he took us to a drug store and let us pick out discounted Christmas presents.

My Aunt Grace wrote a story indicating that my father had no problem being married to a Black woman, but he didn't want to be Black. What did he think his children were? According to my aunt she and my other Black relatives weren't a problem. Although he worked with Chinese cooks and waiters who were allowed to visit our house and spend evenings playing Mahjong, I don't think he wanted to be Chinese either. I think my dad wanted to be all-American, to melt in the pot. Not secretly, like my mother, but just a Chinese immigrant man fitting in. Did race play a part in my mom and dad's divorce or did my mom kick my dad out only because he was a philanderer? According to my Aunt Grace, my father knew nothing about my mother passing for white.

> She [my mother] married a Chinese fellow. He was aware of her background. In fact he said that he wouldn't care to marry a white girl because he felt that they expected a man of a darker race to practically be at their feet. He said they ... always flaunted their (believed) superiority.
>
> But at the same time, he told my sister that he accepted her family, but yet had no intention to becoming a Negro. In other words he did not intend to become assimilated into the race. So she [my mother] felt that the only course left to her was to reject her family (us) and try to hide her background. ...
>
> I accepted her stand. We remained friends even though we did not go to her house openly, but she did to ours. None of us minded too awfully much, we were all busy raising families and did little or no visiting.
>
> Then we bought our house in her [my mother's] neighborhood ... She lived a block down and a block over from us. My oldest boy is very fair and quite blonde. She [my mother] permitted him to come to her house freely.
>
> But Jay, my second son is dark like me, though with beautiful hair and near perfect features. He was not free to come. I was determined that Jay feel no difference and I wasn't going to

have him grow up and say, 'oh yes, they didn't care about me. I was too dark.' ...

Here was my small son, a block and a half away from his little cousin, forbidden to go and play with her. Naturally, I resented it. —Aunt Grace, February 17, 1948 (eleven days after I was born)

Recently, my cousin Jay wrote to me, "We were neighbors in our isolation."

My sister remembers sitting at the top of the stairs to the second floor bedrooms of our four bedroom home listening to my mom and dad yell at each other. I can't remember my dad ever living with us. And, there's not much I remember about my mother.

~ ~ ~

5.

I refused to ~~ix~~ accept her terms that my family should be her admitted inferiors. She made the rules, drew the lines of racial division so I let them stand. My husband has retained his viewpoint. This has all run on for a matter of about four years. Her husband spent two years in the navy, she had a hard struggle. I longed to go to her, but since she had asked us not to come I didn't think there was anything I could do.

Since her husband has been home she has had two little girls, ten months apart, making four girls in all. ~~Afterxxhax xhadx.~~ Right after he came home they bought a larger home in a differnt neighborhood so that our children are no longer going to the same school. That eliminates one phase of the problem.

After her two last babies were born, she lay there for months, unable to walk, with her little six year old and her husband trying to take care of the work and the children between them. I really longed to go to her but was rather ill myself in the last few months of my third pregnancy. Then too, I had said that she put up the walls and that she would have to remove them. I swore I would never go to her unasked. My brownskin sister would have been glad to go but didn't know whether ~~or not~~ she would be given a welcome or the cold shoulder. And yet we all hated to give her up for she was our sister. It wasn't as if she had died. I think that would have been preferable to the situation as it was.

But her illness evidently taught her that her being Chinese didn't ~~help her~~ mean so much. Through her illness she was pretty much uncared for. Her few Chinese and White friends didn't do any too much for her if at all. I think she got rather a new slant on what family could mean to you. At any rate she and her, I should say our, older sister got together and cooked up a sisters' sewing group, mainly for the exchange of ideas.

Mother (1913-1999)

According to the U.S. Census Bureau, in 2012 Black or African Americans were 5.5% of Minnesota's population. (This did not include Blacks or African Americans that claimed to be more than one race.) [4]

I remember Mom wearing cotton print dresses each with a sweetheart neckline and several rows of elastic on each side of the waist to accommodate her girth, dresses she sewed for herself and the neighbor lady. I remember the two of them sitting at our red Formica table, drinking percolated Hills Brothers coffee, eating ginger snaps, or Nabisco Zwieback Toast, and Mom smoking Pall Mall cigarettes.

Sarah Ella Franklin and Daughter

Mom would write me or my sister a note to take to the grocer on 28th Avenue and the grocer would sell us cigarettes. Cigarettes and penny candy. We ate the button candy, the teddy bears, the red hot dollars, NECCO Wafers, the Nonpareils, and Bonomo's Turkish Taffy. We would go to the store and the library almost every day after school. I swear Mom read every mystery book in the library and all the new ones as soon as they were available.

I remember Mom hunched over her Nechhi sewing machine. Pins and needles and patterns spread across our Duncan Phyfe table, cleared only on Sundays to make room for our routine Sunday meals, at noon. Swiss steak. Chicken from a can. Always white rice. Sometimes Boston cream pie or angel food cake. I remember how the angel food cake cooled atop a soda bottle, the

---

[4] http://quickfacts.census.gov/qfd/states/27000.html

pan propped up by chop sticks. I remember how leftover pie dough was sprinkled with cinnamon and sugar and then baked.

I remember Mom peeking out the window between her bedroom and our front porch, vigorously tapping on it to let my sister know it was time to stop kissing her boyfriend and send him on his way. I remember her washing my sister's mouth out with soap and water after the one time she swore.

I remember Mom closing all the windows and shutting the aluminum blinds when an insurance man came to court her after the divorce. She had said, yes, but then changed her mind. We were not to answer the door, but be quiet and not let the man know we were home. She never dated after dad left. I can only imagine how lonely my mom must have been. (I remember her telling me, a few years before she died, how she would like to be with a man, again, just one time; it had been over forty years since my dad. She told me, according to the Bible, it was sinful for a man to be with a divorced woman.)

I remember when our roof leaked and water seeped into the upstairs bedroom I shared with my sister. Mom used her creativity. She painted cardboard pizza circles and nailed them to the ceiling.

I remember when Mom took a hammer to our beautiful built-in wood buffet in the dining room to enlarge the room. She was on a mission. I also remember when she purchased a wall-size mural of mountains and water and trees and pasted it to our dining room wall. Perhaps she was looking for a way, if only in her imagination, out of seclusion.

I remember Mom putting on roller skates, I think she was fifty years old, and skated around our living room, dining room, kitchen, and hallway.

I remember, at the age of fifty-eight, my mother, who had only an eighth grade education, went back to school and got a high school diploma and a business degree. She got a job at a print shop, but retired a few years later because the company went out of business.

Did Mom hug and kiss and praise her children? I don't remember. (I do remember she had a state fair yardstick, and she'd hit me with it until it broke. She wanted to know why I was crying. I was prepubescent. I didn't know why.) Did she make sure we had food to eat and clothes to wear and take care of us when we had the chicken pox? Absolutely, yes. And she read to us. Nursery rhymes. And story books.

Okay, I don't actually remember her reading to me, but I do remember the stories and poems. I remember "The Little Elfman" by John Kendrick Bangs, "There Was a Little Turtle" by Vachel Lindsay, "The Swing" by R. L. Stevenson, and "The Cupboard" by Walter de la Mare." I remember the *Little Golden Book of Poetry* and *Silver Pennies*! *The Five Chinese Brothers. The Country Bunny. Flicka Ricka Dicka. Curious George. The Little Engine that Could.* Yes, and even *Little Black Sambo. The Tinder Box* story by Hans Christian Anderson was one of my scary favorites—the dogs with big eyes!

A friend remembers my mom sitting in front of a fan, always sitting in front of an electric fan in the heat of summer.

Maybe my search for love had something to do with my missing father, but deep in my heart it was my mother I was searching for.

God the Father

My fifties childhood wasn't unusual. Most of my friends were Lutheran and they went to the same Lutheran Church as I did. A few of my friends were Catholic, but didn't live nearby. There were only two of my grade school friends whose parents were divorced, but I don't remember any of us dwelling on it or letting it define us. Yes, I had experienced some childhood trauma. Not wanting to go to kindergarten. Scared of the teachers. Afraid to tell the teacher or the librarian I had to pee and instead peeing on my wee self in shame. But I didn't know I wasn't white, not even sure if I knew I was poor; but being poor and not knowing I wasn't white didn't ostracize me, didn't keep the neighborhood children away from me. Kids liked coming to our home which was a good thing because Mom wanted us where she could keep a close eye on us, where she could protect us.

Our home was lived in. We were allowed to play hard. The carpet was worn, the furniture second hand. Plastic didn't cover our davenport. We had a television and a record player in a cabinet—and my sister and her friends danced! On summer afternoons we set up a card table in the living room and shuffled Mahjong tiles (you could hear the shuffling of tiles a block away) or played Canasta or Sorry or Monopoly.

We had a second hand upright piano on our front porch and we all took turns proudly pounding out "Chopsticks."

In the basement one room had a bar, but no alcohol, just fancy empty bottles and an interesting Econolite motion light with a picture of a young boy peeing. On the other side of the bar room there were shelves and shelves of books. Nancy Drew. The Bobbsey Twins. A Bible written in Chinese. Pearl S. Buck. In the middle of the room we often set up the slide projector or movie projector. We had reels of cartoons and hundreds of slides—many slides were of floats in the Rose Bowl Parade. That is until one day when Mom decided slides and film and books were fire hazards and she threw them all away! The linoleum was pink and blue and consisted of squares with checker boards and squares with nursery rhymes. In the next room there was a shower and a portable steam bath.

In the winter we had a skating rink in our backyard; in the summer we had a sandbox that covered one-fourth of the backyard, and an enclosed playhouse that took up another fourth. We had a stone fireplace to roast hot dogs and marshmallows. In the front yard we played Captain May I and Red Rover Red Rover. We played baseball in the street, only to be kept in when once a year our street was tarred.

Miniature roses and lilies of the valley and peonies and sweet peas surrounded the front and south side of our house.

In second grade my writer's voice appeared from nowhere. I was taught early to be charitable, even though who knew we were the receivers of charity, of turkeys at Thanksgiving and blonde blue-eyed dolls from the Salvation Army at Christmas? I wrote my first poem in second grade: *save your nickels and dimes, Channel 2 needs you, bring your money to school!* My teacher paraded me in front of each elementary school class where I recited my lines and solicited money for a cause, unlike my sister's teacher who hid her in a corner, because, she said, she was so darn tiny, so darn cute (what wasn't she saying).

When the Church solicited money from our neighbors, asking to help the poor family who needed a new roof on their house, the good Christians gave generously. But that money was never given to my mother, and shame burdened my mother until the day she died.

Shame isn't an isolated incident, shame sneaks up on you, says you're not worth shit, and says it over and over and over again—even if you're not listening. Even if it takes a lifetime to name it.

Mother told my sister and me to quit going to Our Redeemer Lutheran Church. My sister eagerly complied. She was more interested in boys than confirmation. But I needed the Church. I needed God, my only father. I needed unconditional love and forgiveness. (And knowing what I know now, I needed community.) But was love and forgiveness truly abiding in Our Redeemer Lutheran Church?

In fourth grade, my Sunday school teacher asked our class if we thought a Black family should be allowed to become members of our Church. I thought, though how could I have known, wasn't I Black, aren't I a member? *Shame.* The family was not allowed to join, but years later, when a new minister arrived, he and his wife touted several adopted Black children. If I was truly white, if I truly blended in as a child, why are my memories so vivid of knowing what I didn't know, and didn't think others knew even though they did?

Confused, but not willing to give up my God, perhaps thinking more religion couldn't hurt, I supplemented my longing by holding a weekly girls' club at our red Formica table, in our yellow kitchen with the red cupboards. Our club was based on Unity's *Wee Wisdom* magazine. I don't remember, but can imagine us nine-year-old girls praying together and drinking Kool-Aid.

I do remember that my mother, a firm believer in the Unity church, sent tithes across state lines so people we didn't know would pray for us. That belief, along with our belief in the power of the planchette moving across our

Ouija Board, brought our family the answers to many prayers. Unity also taught us to *make treasure maps*—visual prayers—as additional assurance that our needs would be met. That's probably what my *Wee Wisdom* Club did, cut and pasted our dreams in the pages of sample books of beautiful, sometimes flocked, wallpaper. (I continue to collage my prayers six decades later.)

In fifth grade my class had a poetry club. (Another community I could belong to.) I was proud to see my words on blue-lined paper, mimeographed so all the fifth graders could read: "pitter patter, pitter patter / the rain does splatter." By sixth grade, however, my pride had sunk. Emotional and physical puberty threw me a curve ball. Although popular enough to be elected student council class representative, I was shy. Instead of going to the playground at recess, I would hunker in the doorway of Standish Elementary School until the bell rang indicating playtime was over. That is until the day the teacher no fifth grader wanted to be assigned to in sixth grade, publically stoned me with her reprimanding words. Shame. How could she not have known what I knew— that no other kids would play with me. That I was different. That each budding sixth grade girl had a guy she was pining for, and a girlfriend to whisper it to. I was not yet budding. And I was pining to be a nun. I wanted to be Catholic. Catholic girls were smart and they were outgoing, and they had been confirmed in fourth grade.

I remained a devoted member of Our Redeemer Lutheran Church and a member of the choir well into my twenties when I no longer lived in South Minneapolis. I also, for a few months, was editor of the Church's newsletter. Once, I even got married in the Church. At first the minister wouldn't marry us because we were living in the same apartment, living in sin. *Shame.* We lied, said we would separate until the wedding, but instead we moved our wedding date ahead, not the usual reason for having a shotgun wedding.

The day of the wedding it rained. The morning of the wedding my husband drank too much wine. After the wedding, my husband and I spent little time at the lovely reception my friend Annie and her mother catered. Instead, my husband spent the evening passed out on the bathroom floor of our apartment; I slept alone in our marital bed.

Eventually, I realized patriarchy was the backbone of the Church and racism was an extended arm, so I ran.

"Here is the church here is the steeple, open it up and see all the [God fearing] people."

Yet, I have fond memories of the stained glass, the liturgy, the music, and my church friends. But I couldn't help but laugh and cry and *praise the Lord* when I discovered that in 2005, Our Redeemer Church was gifted to, and is now home to, an Oromo congregation. Oromo (uh-ROH-moh) people are from East Africa.

If You Want to Sing, Open Your Mouth

Those who lived through the Cold War experienced it in real-time. Rather than concealing developments and events from the public, governments exploited them in the press, on radio and television and in popular culture. The Cold War fuelled some of the most virulent propaganda campaigns in human history. In the West, people were schooled to think the worst of those on the other side of the Iron Curtain; civilians were warned of the possibility of spies, subterfuge and surprise nuclear strikes; school children learned about air-raid drills, bomb shelters and nuclear fallout. It was government agencies that conducted this symphony of nuclear paranoia—but they had willing accomplices among writers, film makers and television studios. The post-war generation, which should have been one of the most prosperous and content of modern times, grew up thinking that the nuclear clock was ticking and that its own destruction may be imminent.

–J. Llewellyn et al, "The Cold War", *Alpha History*

Sixth grade was a year of humiliation and triumph for me, a lonely girl who was starting to realize she was different. She didn't have straight blonde hair and she didn't yet have a menstrual cycle or wear a bra. And, she was told she couldn't sing.

In sixth grade I experienced preferential treatment.

I was told not to isolate myself, to follow the rule that everyone goes to the playground at recess; yet, I was told not everyone could participate in choir— only children with a voice could participate in the school wide United Nations performance. *Shame.*

However, Mother, for the first time I remember, stood up for me. Had she really heard me complain that I wasn't allowed to sing? At the spring parent teacher conference, one of the last she would attend for me (how many conferences can a single mother of five continue to walk to), she confronted my teacher. Maybe she said *it should be about choice, not about talent or skill. Everyone should sing!* I wonder, now, how segregation, how Jim Crow, yes even in the Northern states, might have prompted my mother's concern for equal rights for her sixth grade daughter? Even though she was pretending to be white and hid her children's racial identity, there must have been a fight in her, a line she wouldn't let be crossed that would protect her children with the fierceness only love or the experience of racism could provide.

I remember the day I came home from Sunday School, eager to practice the day's lesson:

> [14] If I then, your Lord and Master, have washed your feet; ye also ought to wash one another's feet. [15] For I have given you an example, that ye should do as I have done to you. [16] Verily, verily, I say unto you, The servant is not greater than his lord; neither he that is sent greater than he that sent him. [17] If ye know these things, happy are ye if ye do them.
>
> John 13:14-17 King James Version

I got a bowl of warm water and a wash cloth and sat at my mother's feet. She was sitting in her rocking chair. She laughed at me and told me to stop— what was I doing? Shame. I always loved my mother. I always wanted her to love me.

My mother said my teacher cried. The next day all sixth graders were told they could sing in the choir if they wanted to participate. I had no choice but to honor my mother's courage, and join the choir. With trepidation, knowing I had no ear or voice for music, I sang.

In junior high the students who had sung in their grade school choirs got to sit in the back of the class—they would be the A and B students. However, my place in the back of the class was temporary. During a choir concert rehearsal, the teacher, pointing his baton, yelled, "Who is singing off tune?" I was transferred to remedial choir. In high school I joined my church choir, loving the music, and the friendships, the green robes. But I only mouthed the words; no one was going to catch me singing off key. Years later, my Aunt Grace said I could sing—I just had to be less timid and sing loud so I could be heard.

1959, sixth grade, was also the year that I remember students at Standish Elementary School practiced what to do if there was a bomb threat. We lined up against Army green walls, crouching, hands crossed behind our bowed heads. I was traumatized. I didn't want to be at school away from my family if a bomb dropped. Also, I panicked because our family didn't have a bomb shelter. I wanted pills that I could carry in my pocket that I could swallow if there was a nuclear attack. I was afraid of being a survivor. I didn't want to witness the aftermath of war. But today we witness it every day on the news, in movies— and we play war games on computers, in warehouses, and out in the field.

1959 was also the year *The Declaration of the Rights of the Child* was adopted by the United Nations General Assembly.

Hunger

Unfortunately, many Americans live on the outskirts of hope—some because of their poverty, and some because of their color, and all too many because of both.

        –President Johnson, State of Union Address (1964)

Beginning in 1954 the U.S. exported food to other countries (Food for Peace); however, in the 1960s the U.S. government decided to also feed needy Americans.

Keeping four girls as pretty as the clothes Mother mostly sewed for us was no easy task, nor was feeding us. Mother didn't drive. We never owned a car after Father left. After Father left we took buses, sometimes cabs, to rummage sales on Chicago Avenue near downtown, or to the Salvation Army Store (and book store) on east Hennepin, the area known as Nicollet Island. Usually we walked, once a week, to Sig's independent grocery store, about six blocks from our home.

When I was too young to help around the house, I wanted to help my mom; I wanted to please her. I wanted to wash clothes with our wringer washing machine, or iron with our electric mangle, and wash dishes, and vacuum, and dust. But when I was older, my teenage years, I lowered my head in shame as I pulled the wire cart full of groceries, across 38th Street, up 26th Avenue, past the homes of my peers. Sig, though, would sometimes give Mother and me and our groceries a ride home in his grocery truck, and for that I was always grateful.

But I don't remember being embarrassed by government subsidized food. My family liked to eat, and I don't remember ever going hungry. We rode buses to downtown Minneapolis and stood in long lines. There was no government cheese back then, but canned meat soaked in what I imagined to be gravy. I loved it over rice. We also received flour, and powdered milk (Mother, thankfully, never insisted we drink the powdered milk, but used it for cooking and baking).

I don't know how we afforded it, but I remember Nestle's Quik with the quirky "N-E-S-T-L-E-S, Nestle's makes the very best... Choc-'late" slogan. I loved using more than I was supposed to so a gob of chocolate would linger on the bottom of my glass. I would dunk buttered (we used Oleo, the kind we had to squeeze the red dot to make it yellow) Wonder bread into my chocolate milk until most of the bread would fall in and become part of a messy mixture of sweet delight! And then there was Tang, the orange powder you mixed with water, introduced in 1959. I think it was the process, the mixing, that mesmerized me.

Recently a friend said she loved my mother's cooking because her mother always overcooked everything. I have never thought about my mother's cooking as being good, but she cooked things we liked, like sloppy Joes—a pound of hamburger could feed the neighborhood, *the loaves and the fishes,* and often did. The only food that made me gag was spinach, didn't matter that it made Popeye strong. But since my sister has taught me to make spinach soup with pork and rice and water chestnuts, my feelings about spinach have gone from yuk to yum!

High school lunches. My most painfully embarrassing job, *shame,* was scraping dishes in the school lunchroom. As my peers passed by, handing me their empty lunch trays, I scraped their waste into the garbage. My pay was free lunches. Contrary to many who complained about the food, I loved school lunches. My favorite was pizza and corn and potato chips!

My friend, Annie, however, whose parents were also divorced, worked in the teacher's lunchroom where she received respect—and tips for her work! Undoubtedly her tip money went to the upkeep of her spiffy blue Mustang that we dragged up and down Lake Street on Saturday afternoons.

Annie's mother vividly remembers three little girls, a blonde, a brunette— and me. She remembers how in high school we would run into the house, put up the ironing board, heat up the iron and ironed our hair. Except you, Sherry, she would always lovingly add to the story. I remember, back in the days, that three were a crowd, and often I was the third wheel or no wheel at all. So it softens my heart to know that everything I think I remember isn't always the truth. But why didn't I iron my hair? It might have been just what it needed.

Besides scraping garbage at Roosevelt High School, I also had the opportunity to work in the school library where G. E. Owens took me under her wing. I didn't realize then that she was only seven years older than me, but I did have a sense we shared a racial identity. I also worked at the Roosevelt Public library. During the summer I worked at a neighborhood settlement house participating in project Play Corps. Volunteers and those of us on the government payroll worked together. We traveled in recycled post office trucks to playgrounds in Minneapolis. We played games and made crafts with the children.

I remember a volunteer who lived in a huge house across from Lake of the Isles (in a wealthy Minneapolis neighborhood). He invited Play Corps staff to a New Year's Eve party at his house. Mother vehemently said no. Was it because I was poor, Black, female, or was I just too young?

Without government *handouts*, for which I am thankful, my story would be a different story.

However, because my mother received Aid for Families with Dependent Children (AFDC), I had to pay my mom room and board out of my earnings, which I didn't mind, but she felt bad about it, shame. My meager support, unfortunately, was then deducted from her aid.

Puberty: Under the Sheets

In 1960, the Federal Drug Association (FDA) approved the birth control pill thanks to two women in their seventies, Margaret Sanger and Katherine McCormick, and biologist Gregory Pincus. McCormick was a major benefactor of Gregory Pincus' research. Margaret Sanger supported using unsuspecting poor women in Puerto Rico as victims of the research. It has also been said that she, as a supporter of eugenics, supported the genocide of Black people.

By seventh grade, 1960, my sister and I stopped wearing identical dresses, she ten months older and spending her time chasing boys. I became political, and acquired the skill of embroidery to embroider blue ribbons with white thread that spelled out the name "Kennedy." I was caught up in the promise of the time, yet I didn't understand why all the excitement surrounding the young Irish Catholic presidential hopeful. However, for a moment, I was experiencing a new community.

But by ninth grade, my sister now in high school, I again felt alone, sad, and afraid. Finally having a menstrual cycle at the age of sixteen, didn't make me feel like a woman, it only caused me embarrassment and shame. My mother, without words of advice or how to, handed me a box of Kotex, a sanitary belt, and plastic panties. I was horrified and ashamed when one day as I led my homeroom class in the Pledge of Allegiance, my teacher took me aside and whispered *go to the bathroom, you are bleeding*. My pale pink dress spotted, bloody evidence that I was now a sexual girl.

I wasn't allowed to use Tampons, though I think my older sisters did. I suspect my mother was afraid a Tampon would lead to other things like knowing my body for the first time, knowing that eventually a man's penis would enter me the same way. Which eventually many of them did, much to my surprise and horror and sometimes joy.

Once, in my thirties, I wrote a poem, "Bleeding to Death," about menstruation. It was published in a book honoring menstruation: Red Flower Rethinking Menstruation by Dena Taylor. The editors, however, edited out the last verse in which I cried out 'damnation.'

At the age of fifty, when the bleeding stopped, except every time I boarded an airplane, my life changed. The change changed me. I no longer planned everything I did around that certain time of the month. I no longer needed to worry if my menstrual blood would betray me.

There were few men in my life (the minister and the fourth grade Sunday school teacher) until junior high school when I finally had male teachers—math and choir, but they weren't mentors, and I didn't have a crush on any of them. The fathers in the neighborhood I stayed shy of, even afraid of—so who was this other sex that caught my attention once I became a woman?

1966. When I was eighteen, my mother knighted me "goody two-shoes." Perhaps a title beholding Cinderella, but a title that offended me. My sister who fret for nothing, high on marijuana or acid or whatever the first wave of Minneapolis hippies were high on seemed beyond Mother's criticism. Just to prove I wasn't all goody-goody, I took half a hit of acid. My sister and her friends  might have been in la la land, but I ended up walking the streets of West Bank Minneapolis in the middle of the night, scared and crying.

Fear kept me from doing some things, but not from doing others.

Mother had insisted I take birth control pills once she discovered my sister was unwed and pregnant. I was stubborn enough to refuse, but eventually gave in and gave up saying *no.* (Although Mother had often threatened she would kill us and the baby too if we were pregnant out of wedlock, it was probably just one of many threats mothers used to put the fear of God in their daughters to no avail. Mom greatly loved her first grandchild. We all did. My sister married the baby's father in the hospital.)

My first sexual experience happened at an unremarkable hippy pad. I slept with an unremarkable hippy. I only knew him by the name of Dylan (no, not that Dylan). We were in the top bunk; my sister and some guy were in the bottom bunk.

But nineteen years old and no longer a virgin, sex was uneventful (it's true we can pop our hymens on bicycles, and I, unknowingly, had in sixth grade.

Mother had asked about the blood spotted underwear, thinking my sister or I had started to menstruate. We both denied the blood was ours. Was she really wondering if I had begun to menstruate, or was she worried about what I didn't know about broken hymens? The underwear was mine.)

Aha! She's Not White

I attended the University of Minnesota (U of M) from Fall 1966 to midway through Fall Quarter 1967. I hadn't planned on going to college, although my senior year of high school I took college prep classes, just in case, and applied to the U of M, just in case. When I graduated high school I was hired full-time at a company punching data into a machine. However, when I received a letter saying I was awarded grants and scholarships, I registered for college.

Spring Quarter of my first year of college, with a counselor's insistence that I would be happier if I lived on campus, and my mother's insistence I wouldn't— how dare anyone suggest her daughter move away from home—I moved into Sanford hall into the only three women dorm room, with the only bathtub, and two women from small towns in Minnesota. Sanford Hall is where I met Carla, who lived alone in a room down the hall from me.

Carla knew me. I didn't have any notion of who she was. I had never known a Black girl before.

I didn't know I was Black. *Why hadn't I met myself?*

Carla would sit in her room on a straight back chair and knead her large breasts *to make them larger* she said, and she said that I *better be doin' something to make my tiny breasts bigger*!

I had never met such an outspoken woman before. Why hadn't I? Even growing up with three older sisters, everything in my family had been secret and fearful. I didn't learn how to love, especially myself.

Carla told me our fathers worked together at the Nankin Café. Was there anything she didn't know? She knew I was so timid I would go without eating instead of going to the cafeteria by myself.

She knew I used expensive white people's hair products on my uncontrollable hair, DuSharme comes to mind; she introduced me to more appropriate products for hair like mine, Black hair products such as Ultra Sheen which I still sometimes use today.

Over the years I lost track of Carla, but I will always remember her for our long conversations about race, about family, and, of course, about men. We also went to a few clubs and a few parties together. (The drinking age in Minnesota was 21 until 1973 when it was lowered to 18 for three years, then raised to 19, and eventually raised back to 21 in 1986; some clubs allowed underage patrons, but they weren't served alcohol.)

However, 1967, nineteen years old, living away from the shelter of my mother's control, I was still naïve about what was happening in the world around me. I didn't know that in July of 1967, the night of the Aquatennial Parade, a riot took place in North Minneapolis—there were fires, arrests, shootings, injuries, and vandalism over a two-day period.

I was too busy looking for love. Under the sheets. As that fortune cookie amusement goes, read the fortune, then add "under the sheets."

"The best thing you can do is get good at being you"
—under the sheets!

Mama's Mother Was a Brown Skinned Girl of Fifteen...

For a better life away from Jim Crow, southern Blacks traveled north searching for opportunity. The Great Migration spanned the early to late 1900s.

Spring 1968. I went to my Aunt Grace's home looking for understanding after my mother criticized me because of an editorial I wrote for my community college newspaper; I was co-editor. I was expecting Mother's pride, instead I received her wrath. How could I publically state that I had smoked marijuana, which I hadn't (not until years later), *shame*. But it wasn't the high I was looking for; I wasn't looking for a false high. My high was God, guys, and a college education.

Grandma Ella Franklin

I respected my aunt's opinion because she had the courage to be a writer. She wrote poems, and stories, and songs—and editorials *regarding the plight of mixed-race children.* She read my college editorial and told me to keep writing. When someone asks me *who my muse is*, I reply, "Aunt Grace." But, recently I have learned from my cousin, my Aunt Grace had her faults. But were they faults or was she a victim of her time? Did being a mother and a wife and a writer—being a Black woman— influence her character, how she often screamed she was going to kill herself? How much am I like my Aunt Grace?

My aunt's poetry was read at her funeral; finally, I thought to myself, some recognition. After her death, my cousin gave me her mother's stories and poems. Amongst them was the beginning of a collection titled *Mixed-Blood*;

coincidently I was in the midst of writing *A Little Mixed Up* (Guild Press, 1982), my first published book of poems.

My aunt's stories were the answer to the question I was often asked, *what am* I?

> Mama's mother [my great-grandmother, Fannie Davis] was a brown skinned girl of fifteen when the red-haired plantation owner's son lured her with a ham and his own char-r-min self. Perhaps, too, she was flattered by this attention. At any rate, Mama [my grandmother, Ella Greer] was conceived and came into the world the only light face among many Black children. She had a rather rough time of it. But her father told her not to be upset by it. ...
>
> As we understand it, the man begged our grandmother to come and live with him and be his housekeeper. As marriage was illegal and verboten, well, this was the way it was done. But Grandma, by now grown as stubborn as she was with child growled, "If you won't marry me, then I won't live with you."
>
> But as a cook for the family Fanny (Grandma) [my great-grandma] had a cabin of her own and could keep the child [my grandma] with her, something like keep and six dollars a month. They were house workers rather than field workers and were fed a little better foods than the field workers. ...
>
> Also Momma [my grandmother] took her meals in the family dining room—but at the children's table. This did constitute some sort of recognition. Her father would coach her and talk to her. The first time he spoke to her he said, "Do you know who I am?"
>
> "Yes," she said, "you're my father."
>
> Later when she became fifteen and made her first marriage to brown skinned Zellie Willson her father begged her to reconsider. "You should think of your children. Don't you want pretty children?"
>
> –Aunt Grace

Grandpa and Grandma Franklin and Child

Papa [my grandfather] came from Chicago, he always said. Momma teased him in her wry way and said, "By the way of____," we don't really know but it seems he came from Virginia. ...

He had watery blue-grey eyes that turned green when he was angry. He was handsome and fair and could be mistaken for any white man anywhere. Then again, perhaps Spanish or Mexican. His hair was dark with wide, smooth waves in it. He had jutting eyebrows over deep set eyes. And always, he wore a handle bar moustache. ...

Papa was a racial mixture. He was the child of a white father and
a negro mother. He was one of ~~the so-called~~ "coffee-colored compromise"
which the Southern segregationist so loudly proclaims that he wishes
to prevent.

Mamma was ~~a tiny~~ as ~~he was huge.~~ ~~He was big and tall or seemed so~~
~~by comparison.~~ ~~I had to look way, way~~ up at him.

His hair was black and curly and his eyes were a clear pale blue/set
in a fine-skinned fair ~~face~~. ~~He had the long-fingered sensitive hands~~
of the artist, ~~that he was~~, for ~~he~~ could sketch or paint anything we
asked of him.

Mamma always asserted that he must have been the son of a big
gambler or a fine Southern gentleman by virtue of the way he loved
to gamble and ~~the way he loved to~~ dress.

Don't misunderstand me. He did not gamble often, maybe three, four
times a year. He had some sort of need to gamble, it was like a fever
with him. His excuse was that he was trying to win a lot of money for us
all. One day when I was about ten I came home from school to find a
lot of pretty clothes spread out on the davenport and the chairs of the
livingroom. There was a blue suede cloth jacket among other things and
a rather babyish little green dress.

I came in, enthusiastic, ~~as was my way~~, embraced my father adoringly and
breathed, "Oh Papa could I have the blue jacket?" What seemed to me
without the slightest hesitation he said gruffly, "Of course baby."

I put it on and went galloping delightedly off to the store.
My sister who was older but tiny got the babyish green dress. "She said,
hurt, "You really got the best thing."

He was the child of a skilled artisan, a wheelwright. No doubt that is where he learned some of his carpentry and furniture building skills. He was living with his mother, a Black woman in a little cabin...

Grandpa Franklin and Cousins

When he was ten years old his mother passed away. So his father took him into the shop with him. There while he was being taught a trade some argument ensued. In his anger he picked up a wheel and hit his father over the head with it. His father, who was rather badly hurt either had him put in jail or else due to his injury was unable to care for the boy so he was imprisoned. After...for a week or more a grizzled Black man asked him why didn't anyone come to see him. "Ain't you got no folks, boy?"

Henry said, "well my mother's dead and I hurt my father."

"I'll git some help fo' ya" the old man said comfortingly. He made a few passes over the boy's head. He was leery of it, knowing little of voodoo. What little he did know of it was not conducive to giving him any ease of mind. So quaking in his boots he stood passively under the old Negro's ministrations.

Within the hour, a distinguished looking gentleman, a judge come to see him.

He obtained the boy's release, then handed him a $5.00 bill. Henry was dumbfounded. Five dollars was like a hundred to his inexperienced eyes. And every one and his brother would be out to take it away from him if they knew he had it.

"Beat your way North boy," said the judge. "And change your name. Your life won't be worth a plugged nickel if you stay around here."

Somehow he made his way to Chicago. We may never in this life know the ins and outs of it. Sometimes he wondered if the old man had died. He wondered if his father perhaps on his bed of pain, or even on his deathbed had sent his friend the old judge to see that he escaped hanging or worse yet even lynching.

He made a vow to never reveal his father's [my great-grandfather's] name and he kept that vow. ...

He finally ended in barrel city. That's where all the lost boys, orphaned or runaways or somehow forsaken, managed to eke out a hardy existence. They lived in packing boxes out behind the packing houses, no doubt living by their wits and hustling what they could.

–Aunt Grace

Who am I? I'm the great-grandchild of Black female slaves and white men. I'm the great American Narrative.

HAIR: not about the hair, but the color of the skin

Every day I must undergo a combing and brushing session, or when at night preparing to wear curls for Sunday School I was wrapped in curl rags.

These were long, approximately one inch strips of torn sheeting. First while you held with a finger the end of the rag on top of your head, a length of hair was wrapped around the rag, then the rag was turned taut around the bottom, and wrapped around the hair until it reached the top of the head. Then the two ends were tied in a hard knot and please believe me they were sheer torture to sleep on.

–Aunt Grace

A few years ago my brother's friend, five years younger than me, told me that his parents told him not to tell anyone in the high school that we both had gone to, that he is Indian. I looked at him in disbelief. I thought I was the only one that was told to keep my identity secret, even though I wasn't sure what my identity was. How many of us were silenced? How many of us were told to pretend we were white? It never dawned on me that everyone knew that I was Black.

My friend Annie said, "we all knew you were Black and were apprehensive, but when you joined our Brownie Troop, everything was okay." Another childhood friend said my mother told her mother, when we were kids, that we were Black; funny my mother didn't tell me! It was my shame, not theirs.

There are few photographs of me smiling. I looked away from the camera; I was shy. Even now I don't like to be photographed (but I have crossed over from introvert to extrovert on the Myers Briggs exam). I see what other people say they don't. I see an ugly girl. Crooked teeth. Bad hair. Glasses. I see skin the color of someone my mother wanted me to be, skin bleached with lemon cream every summer, covered with make-up beginning in seventh grade. *Shame*. I wear it still, I wear it well, and I wear it darker than I did in junior high school because I am trying not to be seen as the white girl. I am trying to express, in any way I can, that despite the Scandinavian neighborhood I grew up in, my father is Chinese, my mother is Black.

However, a few years ago, I experienced straight hair (unlike the straight hair my mom accomplished with home perms and petroleum jelly).

My hair dresser casually blow dried my hair, and then put a flat iron through it. I cried tears of joy. For the first time I saw myself beautiful. At age sixty-three I had long, flat, dark brown hair, highlighted with golden tones—princess hair.

And, yet, why is it when Annie, at our most recent high school reunion, showed me a picture of myself in a group of Brownies, nine years old and dressed in a navy skirt and yellow pinafore, a Dutch style hat on my head, I didn't recognize myself? I asked, "Who is that girl in the front row, the dark one amidst all the others?" Annie said, "That's you." I said, "But it can't be me, my mother would never have let me out of the house with frizzy hair."

It was like a 'fro spilling from the little Dutch cap, and it was like a memory jarring my experience of Vaseline and hot combs over gas flames, and Little Toni "the uncurly permanent" manufactured in Forest Lake, Minnesota, that my mom discovered was similar to a "reverse" perm. No matter, my hair was usually greased down straight and plastered to my head. My mother's way of telling me I didn't have good hair and I believed her. *Shame.*

How disassociated do we become from the beauty of who we are, based on myth? How was having straightened hair as a child different from experiencing straight hair as an adult? And why do hair dressers, and friends, and sometimes lovers like my naturally curly hair better than my straightened hair? And, why, as a child and as an adult, have I always considered my curly hair a curse? Some white people have curly hair.

My mother wanted to protect her mixed-race children. I didn't know then what I know now—the history of slavery in the United States of America. My mother was afraid for her children's safety with good reason. Even my hair had to be disguised.

The early seventies. I spent time at bars drinking wine, lots of cheap wine with a friend I met at work. We both loved short skirts, tall boots—cheap clothes we bought at Target. Both a size three we could wear inexpensive clothes and have them look good on us. We loved dressing up, going out, looking for love. Her light brown hair was thin and a bit unruly. My black hair was thick and more than a bit unruly. We were hip, but not hippies, but we both, for our separate reasons, ratted our hair, believing we had natural afros. Perhaps it was the first time I felt I had the freedom to express who I was, to claim what my mother couldn't, that I was Black.

One night, driving home from a night out at the Depot (originally the Greyhound Bus Depot, then the Depot, then Uncle Sam's, now the First Avenue nightclub) the girl in the front seat, next to my friend that was driving, turned around toward me and asked, "why do you girls wear your hair all ugly like that?"

As often was the case throughout my life, I was surprised by her question, and personally offended. And like so many similar conversations and responses, I said, "I wear my hair this way because I am Black and it's part of my identity." And then, on the freeway, she opened the car door and jumped out. At least, that's how I remember it.

Other Twin Cities' bars I frequented, some more than others (late sixties-early to late seventies) were: Big Al's, Bimbos, Triangle Bar, 400 Club, Viking Bar, The Cabooze, Mr. Nibs, Duffy's / later Norma Jean's, Hexagon Bar, Pearsons, and Star Dust Bowling Alley (area historically known as the 'Hub of Hell'), Red Baron, Buster's, Front Page, King Solomon's Mines/later The Establishment, Cascade 9, Moby Dick's, CC Club, the Gable, Filling Station / Pink Pussy Cat, Stand up Franks, Bunny's, George's in the Park/later Classic Motor Company, Ichabod's, Eddie Webster's, The Rusty Nail, The Wolve's Den, and the Oz.

I remember going with a friend, in the 90s, to pick up her three-year-old son who had been hospitalized. We decided to celebrate his recovery by taking him to have his curly hair cut for the first time. I said let's take him to a barber, telling her about the first time I took my son for a haircut. How the barber sat him on the child's chair on top of the barber's chair and I watched his locks drop to the floor. (After his first hair cut, his curly hair grew in straight. Hair doesn't define who we are.)

It was a cold, snowy morning. We entered a Saint Paul neighborhood barbershop near where my friend lived. High in the barber's chair was a boy with blonde hair, having his hair cut. I was excited for my friend's son to experience the ritual from baby to toddler in this environment where men sit on their throne, making small talk with each other.

The barber ignored us, as if we weren't there. We patiently waited. Finally, he bellowed, "what is it you want?" My friend said, "A haircut like that for my son." Her little boy stood there bundled in his little blue snow suit, the blue hood covering his head. The barber replied, "I don't cut hair like his."

We stood there, silent. Why didn't we respond? Why didn't we scream, *but, you have no idea what kind of hair he has?* Why didn't we, when he said, "the guy across the way cuts hair like his," pull the hood from her son's head and show that his hair was more like his white father's hair, than like his Black mother's hair, not that it should have made a difference? *Shame.*

And angry as we later were, why didn't we contact the Better Business Bureau to report the barber who so boldly refused to wait on a brown baby boy? It wasn't about his hair. It was about the color of his skin, the color of his mother's skin. It was about Minnesota not so nice. It was about injustice and how it angers us, frustrates us, tires us, and humiliates us until sometimes we have no breath left to challenge it.

The same friend and I, a few years later, went to a *we do ethnic hair* salon to get my hair cut. The beautician said *I didn't have Black hair! Maybe I had mixed-race hair.* My friend said I had hair like her mother's—*are you telling me my mother isn't Black?* What is Black? Were they talking about my hair or the color of my skin? *Shame.* Mixed messages. Good hair. Bad hair.

What is my hair? Who am I? Times change. Once I went to a hair salon in North Minneapolis. The stylists didn't question me or my hair. It used to be that one drop of Black blood labeled you Black. Today, one drop of Black blood is not enough and you could be asked to prove yourself. I guess I've been trying to prove myself all of my life.

My mother spent her life trying to keep her Black identity hidden. Even in her 80s, living in a senior high rise, she couldn't admit she was Black. A woman from the center routinely washed and set my mother's hair. One day she braided Mom's hair. Then, she asked my mother if she was Indian. There was a moment of awkward silence. I finally let loose the family secret. "She's Black," I said. I had to remove my mother's braids before she would go down to the dining hall for dinner. *Shame*

.

A House in the Suburbs and a Two Car Garage, Hallelujah

Eventually I moved out of the dorm and dropped out of college because I didn't understand the New Math that was being taught, particularly the use of number bases other than base ten. I didn't know I could have just dropped the class.

For a few months I was employed as a live-in babysitter for a theatre couple's three kids. (The youngest was adopted, a three-year-old Black girl. I took to her as if she were my own. I made us look-alike dresses. I'm sure she never knew how she made me feel at home in my own mysterious identity.) Then, I moved to an apartment on Spruce Place with a small town girl I had met at Sanford Hall.

I registered for classes at Minneapolis Community College, near the apartment on Spruce Place, near Loring Park. I felt more comfortable in the smaller college setting than I had felt at the University of Minnesota. I participated in school activities and socialized. At Minneapolis Community College I met Tom. Tom taught me to smoke cigarettes, drink Scotch, and drive a stick shift.

One night I returned home from a date with Tom and discovered my roommate had locked me out. Earlier that day I had told her I was Black. Thankfully, her biker boyfriend came along, angry at her for locking me out, and coaxed her into letting me in, at least to get my things and move out.

Tom helped me move to my aunt's house in North Minneapolis where I was more than welcome. But I didn't stay long. The song, "Leaving on a Jet Plane" written by John Denver, sung by Peter, Paul and Mary, kept playing in my mind until I boarded a plane for Colorado. My first time on a plane, and my first time away from Minnesota. I was nineteen.

I knew a guy, the tall lanky guy I asked to the Snowball, the only high school formal dance I attended because I could ask a boy (no boy ever asked me), who was, in 1968, stationed in Colorado. I thought I could count on him for moral support and friendship. Instead, I saw him once. He and another soldier took me to a hotel and the rest I choose not to remember.

I moved into the YWCA. And soon after found a sympathetic job counselor, a Mexican woman, who helped me land a summer job at the Denver Mint.

It only took a few weeks for me to feel homesick. I visited a neighborhood coffeehouse, hoping it would remind me of the *Coffeehouse Extempore* in the heart of Minneapolis' West Bank. (The *Extempore* was where, late at night, I would listen to folk singers and watch my sister play *spoons*. Often someone would put soap in the fountain outside the *Extempore* when it was still on Riverside, before it moved to Cedar Avenue, and there would be bubbles everywhere.)

At the Denver coffeehouse I met a hippy. Immediately, I packed my bags and moved in with him, not aware that he was a drug dealer. One night, as we entered a home through a window, cops approached. Luckily we escaped. The next day I escaped the hippy and returned to the YWCA. At summer's end, even more homesick, I returned to Minnesota.

I returned to school that Fall 1968, got a job at a physician's supply company down the street from the school, and eventually, after quitting school and marrying and divorcing Husband Number One, I married Husband Two, my boss at the supply company that rehired me.

1970. Husband Number One was a part-time Themadone (the/mad/ones, bikers that rode Harleys), a full-time national marketing sales rep for an engineering company, and a dad. He was the son of liberal parents; liberal parents who didn't want their son and me to have children because they didn't want any mixed-race grandchildren. Husband Number One had already blessed them with three white grandchildren. Fortunately, for his parents, I was swallowing *the pill*. And, also, our relationship was too tumultuous to even consider making babies.

Husband Number One had been laid off of his job in Minneapolis and was hired by a company in Illinois. Unfortunately, once that company knew all of my husband's business contacts, he was laid off. The afternoon he was laid off, he started drinking. When he drank, which was often, he kept on drinking. We were driving down the road when a cop stopped him. But the cop stopped him for speeding. I said, "Can't you see that he is drunk and he's been driving with one hand on the wheel and beating me with the other?" The cop took Husband Number One to jail, then took me home and asked me for a date!

I didn't press domestic abuse charges; he wasn't charged with drunk driving.

We moved to a suburb outside Boston so Husband Number One could work with his brother. This was our fourth move in less than a year. I became the help. I worked in the office; I also worked in the home where we were living with Husband Number One's widowed brother and two children. I became nanny and cook.

My mother-in-law came to help out when the paid nanny was ready to birth her baby. One night, Husband Number One and I were going to have dinner with his brother and his brother's girlfriend. As I walked down the steps in my floor length, rose-colored velour dress, my mother-in-law, watching me, accused me of wasting her son's hard earned money on clothes. The dress was stylish, but inexpensive. *Shame.*

I ran out the door and into the dark streets of the unfamiliar neighborhood. I didn't understand at the time that *shame* was what I was running from.

I returned home to Minneapolis and sought free therapy because Husband Number One said I was crazy. But, nothing is free. I fell in love with my minister therapist who fell in lust with me. Every day I would sing along with Mary (from the "Jesus Christ Superstar" album), "I don't know how to love him, he's just a man" as I pined away for the married minister who I believed was going to save my life.

One night, the minister asked why I was crying. Before I could answer he said, "You don't have to worry about getting pregnant, I've had a vasectomy." I wasn't worried about having a baby; I was heartbroken that he had a wife.

The counseling session that ended "you're getting better but it will take a long time" ended with me almost dead. I was also attending group therapy sessions at Hennepin County Hospital where I was prescribed uppers and downers, and I listened to people who had lives horrifically worse than mine. Mad at the minister because he wanted to prolong our sessions, most likely to prolong our affair, I swallowed pills by the handfuls.

I confided to the manager of the rooming house I was living in that I had attempted to kill myself. He called an ambulance. At the hospital nurses had me swallow more drugs to counteract the drugs that I had taken, allowing me to live. The next day, the manager of the rooming house I was living in told the minister he was not to see me anymore, not knowing the minister had already told me he couldn't see me anymore because I would damage his professional credibility.

The next day, my doctor asked me if I was going to do it again. I said, "No" and was released. I didn't know I would. Nor did I know the minister wouldn't be the last minister (and later there was the professor) I would have sex with. Nor did I know then, what I know now, that I was an innocent victim of men with way too much power and a lot of manipulative charisma.

Eventually I learned Husband Number One wanted to marry a woman in California who had a father. Instead of admitting he was in love with someone else and wanted a divorce, he had chosen to vilify me.

Eventually I moved to Colorado with the manager of the rooming house I was living in, who saved my life. I had unfounded suspicions, gut feelings, that this man was too good to be true. But, my Aunt Grace liked him. And, he did give me a gift of a poetry book by Rod McKuen, and vowed to marry me. So off I went. Unfortunately, I discovered, after a few months in Colorado, that my suspicions about the man I was with were true.

He disappeared, leaving me alone in our apartment in downtown Denver, when he realized that once the Christmas cards I sent from Colorado arrived in Minneapolis with our new address, the hunt for him would be over! He left a note: *I didn't mean to hurt you.*

A woman in the apartment building I was abandoned in graciously accepted some of my belongings. She shared her own story of abandonment, a story about a perfect husband, community man, and church man aka mobster.

My neighbor and I sat in my apartment, lights out, watching out the window. There was a car idling across the street. After ten or fifteen minutes, the driver drove around the block, then returned, drove around the block, then returned, drove around the block then returned. My neighbor said, "FBI."

Earlier, I had called my friend who worked in the Minneapolis Police Department and she said the guy I was with was wanted for stealing a car in another state and for stealing all the rent money from the rooming house that I had lived in. When she had seen my name associated with the felon, she told her colleagues it couldn't be true because she knew me, and knew I wouldn't be with a felon—but, unknowingly, I was. I called the FBI at the number my friend had given me. The agent who responded seemed not to care. Yet, there was a car outside of my window and someone in it was watching my apartment. I don't know why the driver didn't knock on my door. I would have offered him coffee.

In less than a week everything I owned was given away or trashed—how many times have I lost everything because of a relationship? Thanks to Traveler's Aid, I got on a bus and headed home. I arrived in Minneapolis on Christmas Eve. To avoid disrupting a family holiday gathering, I went to a downtown bar, met a guy who was also transient, and together we celebrated, drunk and depressed.

The next day, after a night in a seedy motel, I called a friend. She invited me for Christmas dinner and offered me a temporary place to stay. I got a present that night in the basement in the dark. At first I thought it was the dog slobbering me with his tongue. It wasn't. Well it was, but it was also my friend's father (my friend was living with her parents), who had sauntered away from his matrimonial bed, fondling me. My friend wasn't offended or surprised when after some nervous hesitation, I told her about the situation. Her father, she said, often asked her to drive him to the nearest massage parlor (call it what you want) late at night, usually after he had been drinking.

1973. Husband Number Two. Marriage, the fairy tale concept little girls are brought up to believe—even now in the twenty-first century, which disturbs me— was probably why I clung to my second marriage as long as I did. It was evident from the beginning I had entered a realm of *pure imagination* having won the golden ticket. I thought marriage was love, was acceptance, and that being married meant I was okay. It was none of those things.

Again, I married into a wealthy and refined family. When I met Husband Number One, I didn't know how to cut steak with a knife. I still laugh every time I remember our first dinner date—steak flying off my plate and across the room. *Shame.* And the first time I had dinner at my second set of in-laws' home, I panicked as I attempted to peel potatoes. *Shame.* To this day, when I peel potatoes, I lose as much potato as potato skin. Food is story about culture and class. Our family ate white rice, always rice—no need to peel or slice.

Mealtimes with Husband Number Two and his parents were seldom the quality family time they should have been. There was less conversing, at least on my part, than shock and dismay. "It's bad enough to have to hire a woman," my father-in-law, a vice president for a Fortune 500 company, bluntly stated," but I would hire a woman over a Negro any day."

Pregnant with Son Number Two

My in-laws were not told I was Chinese and Black. Husband Number Two had once been engaged to an African American woman and he was immediately disowned from any inheritance his father would eventually leave him. To this day, I wonder if Husband Number Two married me to deceive his father. By that time of my life, mid-twenties, resignation was my way of living. I said, "Tell your parents whatever works for you." So Husband Number Two told his parents I was Polynesian.

I grew up with my mother's insistence that I would marry a white man, whether she said this directly or not. *South Pacific*, the movie, 1958, was a family favorite.

I fell in love with (Tonkinese) Bloody Mary and the (white) lieutenant and hoped and prayed the lieutenant would marry Bloody Mary's daughter, Liat (and my mother hoped and prayed my sister would marry the guy she was dating who looked like the lieutenant—but the mother of my sister's boyfriend was not going to let her son be with a Black girl, although he eventually married someone Chinese). I wanted to marry Rossano Brazzi! Ensign Nellie Forbush, who wasn't carefully taught, certainly didn't deserve Emile De Becque—but I, a young girl seeking a father figure, one less abstract than God the Father, did!

When I showed the film to a group of eleventh and twelfth grade students in 1997, they fidgeted in their chairs, laughing at the musical, and my attempt to lead a discussion fizzled. Was it uncool to let their peers know that they knew the movie from 1958 might have relevance to them?

I was happily married to Husband Number Two for seven years. I was *Harriet* because I had finally found *Ozzie*—but, I was also *woman* and could do everything and I did: I raised two toddlers, cooked and cleaned, coddled a husband, went to church, worked full-time, attended college part-time, and wrote poetry. However, the book of poems I wrote and typed and photocopied on yellow paper, and gave to friends at Christmas, was, looking back, a testimonial that Ozzie and Harriet's marriage was knee deep in muck.

The Lutheran church we attended was embroiled in controversy. There were the staunch conservative Lutherans and those who passionately spoke in tongues, praising the Lord with their wild antics. Husband Number Two was ambivalent. Once in a while he reluctantly joined our friends and me for Sunday evening prayer and praise services, but he was confident that choir practices on Wednesday evenings and Sunday morning services were enough to keep him in God's good grace.

Once Husband Number Two and I attended a charismatic service at Met Stadium with thousands of flailing Born Again Christians. The event didn't move my stoic husband to wave his arms in the air muttering holy petitions, nor did the Holy Spirit move me to speak in tongues (as much as I prayed for the experience), but the emotional outpouring of the masses did make me feel like I could move mountains.

In order to do so, though, I had to burn my past. Afraid a fire would burn down our baby blue rambler, I prayed that throwing letters and gifts from former boyfriends, along with any devilish books or music that I owned, into the garbage would be good enough. Along with the trash went Helen Reddy's album and my belief that I could do anything gone, but also my nightmares. Eventually I quit my marriage to my church, and to my husband.

I quit the church when a well-meaning friend sighed, "I wish I could just stay home from church one Sunday morning, and sleep in, but I am afraid I won't go to heaven when I die." How easy it is to be brainwashed by religion, by movies, by music, by mothers, by television—by Cinderella and Snow White.

But quitting church was easier than quitting a marriage, quitting eight years of pretending the middle-class life style was working for me. I had already quit one marriage, being told I was crazy and needed therapy. Didn't dawn on me then that racism and sexism and classism had begun to complicate my life and shatter my dreams of unconditional love. But having two beautiful brown skin baby boys made me come to my senses.

Between my four siblings and I there have been sixteen divorces.

Sons

The day that my friend's blonde three-year-old came home from nursery school and said, "I don't understand, Roosevelt is Black and mean, but Michael is Black and nice," that I realized I couldn't continue the debilitating charade that allowed me to have an *Ozzie and Harriet* life.

At age three, Michael's darker skin had already marked him as other. I remember reading him a story about the United Nations and he pointed to a Chinese woman and he said she looked like my sister, and I said you are Chinese too, and was surprised by his defiant response, "no I am not." Later, when I told my son he is Black, he, again, defiantly said, "no I'm not." But later he said it was okay, he loved me.

I wonder if it was wrong for me to read my sons the book *Epaminondus* by Sara Cone Bryant, over and over again, as it had been read to me as a child, until they had memorized one of their favorite stories, the first story they learned to read. Did my mother, did I, see ourselves as "mammy"; did my sons see themselves as ugly and stupid? Did the book harm us, influence us negatively? We loved the story. But I won't pass it on to my grandchildren.

When anything Black became negatively associated with my younger son Michael, *shame,* I told Husband Number Two it was time to tell his parents the truth that I wasn't Polynesian and their grandsons were not Polynesian. But like many discussions of race with white people who exclaim, "but I'm not racist" or "I didn't have anything to do with slavery," Husband Number Two's response was "you know I'm not racist, except Indians, they are all drunks, but that's not being racist, that's just how it is. And, my parents love you, why tell them you are Black and not have them love you anymore?" *Shame.*

Because Husband Number Two wouldn't tell his parents, I took it upon myself to write the in-laws a letter. Although he wouldn't write the letter himself, he wanted to see what I had written, but I refused. Much to my surprise, my mother-in-law quickly responded saying they loved me as a daughter, and they weren't as naïve as I probably thought they were. But, it was too late. And I ran as fast as I could from our three bedroom rambler, two car garage in the suburbs. Unfortunately, I left without the two children I was trying to protect.

I wonder how easy it is for my sons, now in their thirties, to straddle the lines between Black and white, rich and poor (though they didn't grow up poor). They have both married white women from small towns outside the Twin Cities. How does their knowledge of being mixed-race affect them? I was afraid to meet their in-laws, to attend baptisms in their churches, afraid that who I was would interfere with my sons' happiness. Because I grew up passing for white, living a lie, I wanted my children to know the truth, *you are Chinese and Black and German and Bohemian.* What they did with that knowledge was up to them.

When Husband Number Two remarried, he adopted his second wife's two girls who are close to the same age as our two boys. All the children taunted Michael, even his brother. How did the taunting affect Michael? Was the fact that he was bullied also the reason he was punished, over and over again, for being slow, for not living up to the parents' expectations? In grade school, Husband Number Two and his second wife sent Michael to a therapist.

One day Michael, then four or five years old, said to me, "Mom, I like Michael Jackson, he has my name and he is the same color as me." I found a Michael Jackson outfit, plain black pants and a blue shirt with some black trim, and sent it to his father for him. His father sent it back to me declaring his son was not going to wear Michael Jackson clothes!

Was it really about the clothes? Infuriated that Husband Number Two deprived our son of a positive experience, I asked for mediation. The mediator asked that all of us, Michael and his brother and I and their dad and their stepmom, come together to sort things out. However, at the time of mediation the mediator couldn't remember that she had asked the boys to be there and sent them out of the room. I felt ambushed. The discussion ended when

Stepmom explained that she told the children that Michael is Black because he tans darker in the summer. Problem solved. The mediator sent everyone home.

From that day on, I struggled to find a way to reverse our joint custody. Husband Number Two had physical custody during the school year, and I had custody every other weekend and all summer. (My lawyer wanted me to keep the house and primary custody of the children, but I couldn't imagine earning enough money to pay for a mortgage and support my sons, and I wanted the boys to stay in their neighborhood and their school with their friends.)

Five years later, when I married Husband Number Three, Husband Number Two,

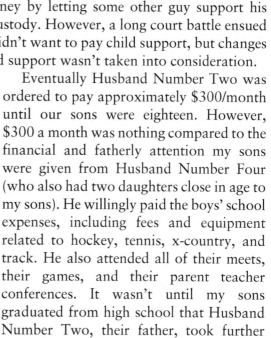

thinking he could save some money by letting some other guy support his children, agreed to a reversal of custody. However, a long court battle ensued because Husband Number Two didn't want to pay child support, but changes in custody weren't allowed if child support wasn't taken into consideration.

Eventually Husband Number Two was ordered to pay approximately $300/month until our sons were eighteen. However, $300 a month was nothing compared to the financial and fatherly attention my sons were given from Husband Number Four (who also had two daughters close in age to my sons). He willingly paid the boys' school expenses, including fees and equipment related to hockey, tennis, x-country, and track. He also attended all of their meets, their games, and their parent teacher conferences. It wasn't until my sons graduated from high school that Husband Number Two, their father, took further interest in them and has helped to support them financially.

LOVE IMAGINED another frog, and another frog

Remember those t-shirts from the 70s, the ones imprinted with "love sees no color"? Even I bought them, but I no longer buy their message. I can't imagine love that doesn't see color. I refuse to be invisible. You can't love me if you don't accept that I am colorful.

If I hadn't always married white men, would it have made a difference?
Ex-Husband Number One apologized for having been a drunk and wanted to date me after his third marriage ended. Instead he met a woman online, an African American woman who, like him, rides motorcycles. Ex-husband Number Two is the father of my sons—we are cordial despite the fact I divorced him because he wouldn't tell his parents I am Black and Chinese (yet now he has a Vietnamese grandson). Alas, Ex-husband Number Three packed his bags and moved out one weekend when I was at a creativity retreat for women—his note said I had driven him crazy; no doubt I had. However, I will always be thankful that our marriage is what allowed me to gain physical custody of my sons. Ex-husband Number Four and I are still friends, although

the reasons I divorced him haven't changed. He recently admitted he just might have an Asian woman fetish. Geeze, I just happen to be an Asian woman. His daughters thought, after twelve years of knowing me, I was Japanese. Politically he is right and I am left.

White boys. In college I dated a guy whose parents didn't like that I was Black, but after graduation he went into the Peace Corps and met and married a woman from South America.

I dated another guy whose parents weren't keen on my being mixed-race, but he went to Japan and met and married a woman from Japan.

Sometime after my first marriage I was engaged to a Moby Dick's (bar that was on Hennepin Ave) foosball groupie, but after we received counseling and the blessing of his minister, and had invitations printed, he decided to marry his white cousin who had a mixed-race child.

People of color. I dated a Black man from Chicago, once. He liked to take photos of women's butts and wasn't interested in a deeper relationship. My mother found out and was furious. Not about the butt photos (I don't think she knew about the photos), but furious that I was dating a Black man.

I dated a Mexican with three children. One day he just decided it was over. His eight-year-old eldest daughter, daddy's caretaker, and I held each other crying.

I met a Chinese man via online dating. He adamantly and repetitively told me his family grew up in Minnesota and they were Minnesotans. You betcha! He didn't know anything about his Chinese heritage and didn't want to know.

I dated a Native American man once, but the fact I had a graduate degree seemed daunting to him, though in many ways he is much smarter than I am.

I had a three-year relationship with a Chicana woman. I thought, fairy tale ending: two women/two women of color! At San Francisco pride she sat with her mother, behind me. I felt We were invisible, not partners, merely individual spectators. Someone told me two women of color in a relationship can have a difficult time because inevitably they each would bring their personal history of racism and sexism into the relationship. I later realized a narcissist and a caretaker don't make for good company, either!

I dated a Black male writer with a foot fetish, what Cinderella wouldn't be acceptable to that, but he chose not to be in a long distance relationship.

Recently at a birthday celebration dinner for one of my friends, I was again the only one without a partner, but I noticed all my colorful friends were with white partners.

Fear

Writing and talking about race and how it has affected me scares me. Honestly, I am afraid of consequences. My mother had her reasons for hiding us; I believe she feared for our lives. I believe she knew we could be killed. I believe she said our neighbor had a gun.

1982. I received an anonymous envelope in the mail. In it was a copy of a newspaper article Barbara Flanagan wrote for the Star Tribune. In the article she had written that I was *a little mixed up,* the title of my first book. The envelope also contained photocopies of articles and pictures of mixed-race couples and children. It included typewritten notes including:

> Hitler brainwashed the Germans into thinking it was alright to destroy the Jewish race, now we have our government and churches brainwashing our American citizens into thinking it is alright to destroy God's created races through sex-relations and producing mixed race children for future generations of America. Have we not had enough of Satan's freedom to destroy? ...

> A child has the God given right to be born of a pure race, just as our Lord intended it to be. ...

> God created the pure race people, sinful man created the mixed-race people.

Who would write and send such bigoted propaganda? It must be a crazy person, I thought. This crazy person has my mailing address. Is this crazy person going to shoot me? Was I wrong to write my story?

From the moment that I opened that malicious mail, and for weeks and months later, I was afraid. But, in 1988, six years after I received the mail, Elroy Stock, who sent thousands of such letters, was exposed.

The same year I received the mailing, I had conducted a writing workshop that resulted in the book *Chromosomes and Genes* which included photos and stories and poems of people of mixed identities. I dedicated the book to my Aunt Grace who had written:

I am in fact one of the racial mixtures who has no roots, found no anchor, gained no secure place or feeling of belonging. I am an outsider....I belong nowhere. It hurts me to say it. It hurts me to think it, and yet it hurts me to live it too.

However despite the fear, the pain, and the shame We survive. Robert Coles, in the forward to *Voices from the Whirlwind an Oral History of the Chinese Cultural Revolution* by Feng Jicai wrote:

As one reads these remembrances, one yet again realizes that our lives are not given shape only by the early childhood we happen to live, or even the particular social and economic world we inherit from our parents and grandparents. A nation's ups and downs, its political history, can become the ruling force upon the lives of thousands, millions of men, women, children.

He continues:

Yet, amid such awful circumstances, amid so much wrong-doing and evil, amid a kind of panic and wickedness of vast proportions, and for a while, of seemingly endless duration, any number of vulnerable men and women and children managed to survive—not only survive in body, but in mind and soul.

MENTOR but David Mura will be teaching in the spring

When I was in graduate school, 1994-1996, there were no professors of color teaching in the MFA program. When I complained, I was told *David Mura will be teaching a seminar in the spring*. Unfortunately, when I went to register for David's class, following the process we always followed to register for classes, I was told that the class was full and there was a waiting list. I was furious. *Shame*. What to do, what to do. *How could I not be included, I am the only student of color in my graduate program*. The response: *no you're not, there's so and so*. The student that was being referred to was an international student, but why didn't I know her, why had we never met? I emailed students and faculty throughout the English program. Some students replied with a disturbing, so *what*! The director said rules change; it is what it is, too bad, put yourself on the waiting list.

I called Mr. Mura. He didn't particularly welcome my call, but was surprised by my concerns. He said he thought he was to be responsible for choosing class participants based on their writing samples. Eventually, through his intervention, I and others were admitted to the class and others were dropped. David called to tell me I got in, but wanted me to know it wasn't like he was doing me a favor; I can't remember his exact words.

A strange and uneasy, for me at least, academic relationship commenced between me and David. But I understand now, having taught for more than a decade, how WE are always under scrutiny, always aware of our every action, our every word, no matter how recognized and honored we may be for our work. We are always on guard.

One day in class David handed me, under the table, a notice about a Writer's Bloc program sponsored by the Asian American Renaissance with a note asking if I was interested. I was. David's, albeit subtle, gesture provided an opportunity that changed my life. I learned how to mentor and teach young Asian writers in community settings and high schools. I participated in a thriving Asian Arts community, a vast community of Chinese, Indian, Korean, Japanese, Vietnamese, Hmong, Tibetan, and other Asian artists. Eventually, I was hired as the Youth Program Manager and was volunteer editor for their annual journal.

David's graduate seminar was a positive experience and much appreciated. David shared poetry and prose by authors I would not have been introduced to in most of my graduate school classes. He created a safe, and challenging, and oftentimes fun experience. Shannon Olson was in our class and quite funny as she performed her spoken word performance and I am happy that her final project became a well-known first book, *Welcome to My Planet: Where English Is Sometimes Spoken*. I was probably not so funny, but loved my group's feminist retelling of the *Wizard of Oz*, because, of course, I wore red high-heeled shoes!

Eventually, after graduate school, I approached David to mentor me. He was reluctant to accept payment, but we both knew artists deserved to be paid, and we were entering a contract, not as friends, but as a professional writer to a beginner writer struggling to write a book. My book, *Chinese Blackbird*, was completed and published by the Asian American Renaissance because Elsa Battica, Director at the time, insisted on publishing it. In 2008, it was re-published by Modern History Press, Ann Arbor Michigan.

I will always be grateful for David's honest feedback and his insistence that I have stories that need to be told. His mentoring gave me the encouragement I needed to keep writing. David wrote: "And after you read this book [*Chinese Blackbird*], if you have any sense at all, this woman is a hero. This book is a gift. ... It will tell you how complicated a thing it is to grow up in this country as a person of color with a mixed racial and cultural heritage."

2008. David Mura and I both had books published with the word "suicide" in the titles. When I finished reading David's book, *Suicides of the Japanese Empire*, I felt I had just read my story, not my exact story but the emotional essence of my story. His novel read, for me, like memoir.

David told me, after he read my MFA final project, that my project was an outline for several books and that he didn't care if I wrote it as fiction or memoir, just write it, and don't burn it as I had planned to do (I didn't burn it, but I left it in a house in Seattle, good as gone.)

Eventually, I began to write my story as memoir, *Love Imagined*. Over many years I struggled with the writing. One night I picked up the almost forgotten manuscript and read it aloud, drinking scotch on the rocks as I read, and I cried, and cried, and cried. Looking back at my life was quite emotional. The next morning, quite sober, I hurried to my computer wondering, did I really mail my manuscript to how many people? I had. But, David was one of the first to respond and he said, *keep on writing*.

A MASTER'S EDUCATION or because she was a nigger

> and when we speak we are afraid
> our words will not be heard
> nor welcomed
> but when we are silent
> we are still afraid.
> So it is better to speak
> remembering
> we were never meant to survive.
>
> Audre Lorde

The seminar was *Breaking Silence*. We were a class of about thirty students. We studied people who had courageously broken their silences; along the way some students also broke theirs. I, however, along the way, was silenced.

It was a hot humid day. We were discussing *The Color Purple* by Alice Walker. The professor asked, "Why would Sofia respond to the governor's wife in anger? Didn't she know the consequences for a Black woman refusing a white woman's request?" Silence, for just a second. And then, a student shouted out, "Because she's a nigger." Silence, just for a second. And then, the professor replied, "well, besides being a nigger?"

The dialogue continued as I looked around the room for some glimpse of outrage, some spark of recognition that what had been said by both student and professor was offensive. It was a teaching moment that didn't happen.

I was angry. *Shame*. Angry at what I had witnessed. Angry that no one was outraged. Angry that I was so outraged I couldn't speak. Silenced by the shock of the silence. I couldn't say what the professor herself should have said.

> The young unkempt woman still in her pajamas shuffled into her 8 a.m. college psychology class and sat down next to Barbara Douglass.

> 'I'm sure glad there are no niggers in this class 'cause I can smell them a mile away,' the young woman declared.

– 81 –

'There must be something wrong with your nose,' Douglass replied, 'because one's sitting right next to you and you can't smell me.'

Although Barbara Douglass never told anyone she was white, people see her porcelain skin and her silky hair and assume she is.

–Monica L. Haynes, *The Pittsburgh Post-Gazette*.[5]

They say not to take everything personally, but *they* are wrong—it is personal. I feel it in my body. *The body tenses. The heart beats faster. The stomach aches.* The best I could do was to later email the professor with polite indignation.

Her response was, "well, you understand what I meant to say."

White people… can go through their life without ever having to talk about race. People of color, however, do not have that privilege. For people of color, silence means that we lose something. It means that we are helping to keep our stories invisible.

– Nashalys Rodriguez and the Contemporary Racism blog.[6]

I have never been able to write an essay. Comments on my final MFA twenty-book essay included the fact that it was courageous of me to write a non-linear essay, but my attempt failed. *Shame.* I hadn't been trying to write a non-linear essay.

Don't you think it's amazing
that you passed me
on the M.F.A. Essay Exam and
accepted my final M.F.A. Project
as proof of earning
a graduate degree?

Did you know my final g.p.a.
is 4.0?

And do you know
I am Black/Chinese?

–Sherry Quan Lee, *Chinese Blackbird*, "MFA"

---

[5] http://old.post-gazette.com/lifestyle/20031026stain1026fnp2.asp
[6] http://contemporaryracism.org/770/social-consequences-of-breaking-the-silence/

Hidden in a hotel room for a week, crossing every "t," looking up every ostentatious word to make sure I was using it correctly, I wrote my final exam. I looked up the word "incredulous" which happened to present itself to me (words do that, come knockin' on my door, words that I have never heard before), but despite my effort to understand the word and use it correctly, I apparently, made an *incredulous* mistake.

> A Student explained that only 15% of us will move outside the economic class we were born into. How disheartening! The reason is, she explained, that people stay fixed in the language of their families. My family spoke in tongues that couldn't be deciphered by the white folks in our neighborhood. Unfortunately, they couldn't be deciphered by us, either. My second cousin and I agreed that we have learned new language in the academy that allows us to know our experience as mixed-race light skin Black children. How strange is that? And, now that we have learned all about oppression from mostly white women scholars, what do we do with all that learning?
>
> –*Black White Chinese Women Got the Beat*,
> performance by Sherry Quan Lee and Lori Young-Williams

I went to graduate school to prove to myself I could. To be the first in my family to earn not only a Bachelor's Degree but also a graduate degree, and to be a role model for my sons. (I didn't know then, that my uncle had earned a Bachelor of Science in Electrical Engineering Degree at the University of Minnesota in 1947, a year before I was born.)

I *worked twice as hard*—only to be told I was *incredulously* wrong.

(At my graduation party some party goers were upset that the cake, which a friend had ordered for me, didn't acknowledge that I am also Chinese. The words were from a poem I had written. We are always under scrutiny—by others, by ourselves.)

THE GIRL WHO CRIED UNCLE if it walks like a duck

Edmond G. Franklin (1917 - 2005)

My uncle lived in Ohio with his wife, Doris. He, like my mother, chose to pass for white. When I was in college, I wrote to him asking if he would share some of my mother's family stories because she wouldn't, she couldn't.

He replied, "I am not fully in sympathy with your trying to find out who you are by delving into your genetic history."

He wrote:

> You might say that I'm often what is called 'passing for white'. Did you ever hear the old story about 'if it walks like a duck, if it talks like a duck, and it swims like a duck—it must be a duck'? Well-if a person talks like white middle class, acts like white middle class, in general he will be treated like white middle class.

However, Aunt Grace, Edmond's sister wrote:

> There are those who advise 'You don't look like a Negro, you don't talk like a Negro and you don't act like one. In fact there is nothing about you to remind us that you are a Negro—so why don't you just forget it.' This sounds simple but in practice it doesn't work. It is just like saying 'Kill your grandmother and forget her!'

Uncle Edmond said his wife had "a lot of books around since she retired—including books about Negro poets" and did I want some of them. And if I wanted to visit, he would pay my plane fare.

> Dr. Doris Franklin, uncle Edmond's wife, was also highly accomplished. She taught at Kent State and received a Distinguished Teaching Award in 1959. She earned her bachelor's degree, and PhD in Philosophy at the University of Minnesota and was an editor at the University Press. She was a member of Phi Beta Kappa.

> In 1967, Doris Franklin, along with 34 other Kent State faculty, signed an anti-war letter and petition addressed to President Johnson to stop the Vietnam War. The letter, along with the signatures, was a full page in the Cleveland Plain Dealer paper.

> In April 1970, the United States, under the presidency of Richard Nixon, invaded Cambodia for the purpose of attacking Viet Cong headquarters. On May 4, 1970 four students were killed and nine injured at Kent State by Ohio National Guardsmen. Dr. Franklin wrote most of the unpublished report detailing the university's Commission on KSU Violence investigation into the May 4th shootings.

Uncle Edmond wrote:

> Dear Sherry: Thanks for your letter. I found it and your books rather interesting. ...
>
> Let me explain what I have done to myself. I have had stomach ulcers, back trouble, and tension headaches that went on for years. But I finally realized that other people were not doing this to me-I was doing it to myself!
>
> I have fought my way through life. Starting with my mother who told me I might as well get out and learn how to shine shoes ... to some well-meaning but misguided high school teachers that wanted me to go to a Black college in the south, so I could be with my people. ...
>
> The point I wish to make is that you may find consolation in the company of others of mixed blood but most of us must live and compete in a so called white world. I'll grant you that I don't advertise my race. ...
>
> Any Black with intelligence can get a college degree and a really good career. Of course he can't get into some country clubs and his children will be called 'nigger' by jealous and mentally twisted people, but who the hell cares!
>
> But this is a hell of a way from picking cotton for a living and living in a one-room shack heated by a fireplace (that also served as a stove), as my grandmother did, or working as a Pullman porter or a coal bearer as my father did.
>
> Yes, I think of my heritage. I think of my Black grandmother that loved me and kept me from dying when I was a child sick with colds and worse. But-grandmother knew better than to fight the southern system. As they say, 'she voted with her feet' and came to Minneapolis and paid to bring her daughter (my mother) to Minneapolis too.

–Excerpts from letter to me from Edmond Franklin, undated.

Dear Sherry:

Thanks for your letter. I found it and your books rather interesting; however I must say at the outset that I am not fully in sympathy with your trying to find out who you are by delving into your genetic history. Each of us is a unique creature — none of us are alike (except identical twins) no trees, fish, birds or insects are alike — all are slightly different. (Some scientists actually speculate that even electrons and atoms may not be really all alike)

First, I gather that you are concerned with so called racial differences. Perhaps you know that there is only one ① human race even though lots of people talk of the white race, the black race etc. It is not true — just as all dogs belong to the canine race — whether they are black, white, curly haired, short legged or otherwise — so all men belong to one race and the differences between men are much less than say those in the race of dogs. The slight differences in skin color — hair texture, and facial structure are really very minor, (incidentally I believe Ruth Benedict says less than 10%)

I'll grant you that a part of the predominant racial group — which we call whites — are biased about race and have not only abused other

[americans are free from any negro blood]

- 88 -

I had only known my uncle by the money he sent to Mom and my aunt each year at Christmas. (I don't think he started sending the money until my mother and my aunt were living in public housing; and, I don't know if he sent money to any of his other siblings.) My mother always divided the money between me and my siblings. When Mom died, he sent the money to me, a thousand dollars, which I shared with the siblings who would accept it.

But after a couple of years the money and the Christmas cards stopped. Eventually, I received a phone call from an attorney who said a neighbor had discovered my uncle and his wife, both senile, living in filth amongst their many cats.

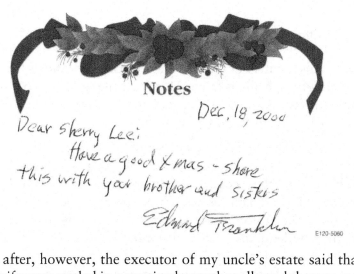

Notes

Dec. 18, 2000

Dear Sherry Lee:
Have a good Xmas - share
this with your brother and sisters

Edmund Franklin

E120-5060

Soon after, however, the executor of my uncle's estate said that my uncle and his wife were settled in a nursing home that allowed them to stay together, and they were doing well since they were on medication.

I wish I had visited my uncle before he died. I wish I had been more understanding of who he was and how he chose to live his life. But I wonder if happiness can only be achieved with lies and deception, or if the true deception is that happiness is impossible to achieve and the purpose of life is merely to survive.

I was the first Black student to graduate with an MFA degree in Creative Writing from the University of Minnesota, although I was probably tracked as Chinese and thus the distinction of first Black graduate went to a friend, a few years after I graduated. My uncle earned an engineering degree; I wonder if he was tracked as white?

Uncle Edmond wrote:

> I made it through two years of college on an aid program called NYA [National Youth Administration]. I was paid $20 per month [25 cents an hour] to do work in the physics lab and I had to walk from 36th and Chicago south to the U because I didn't have car fare (after books and tuition) winter and summer and the worst part was crossing the river bridge with the wind howling. But as the old saying goes 'struggle makes us strong!' I have no use for anyone today that can't make it through the university now with all the help and aid that's available.

> I realize that your struggle was different from mine in many ways. My father-though he was an alcoholic and a gambler-never left his family, but I realize that I learned two things from him that outweigh all his faults. He taught me to 1) keep out of trouble with the law and 2) to work hard. (I never forgave your father for leaving his family.)

In 2006 the University of Minnesota's School of Physics and Astronomy's newsletter reported that Edmond G. Franklin had donated two million dollars for physics scholarships, the second largest in the school's history. Edmond was a student of Alfred Nier. During the war years my uncle worked on the Manhattan Project (the project that created the Atomic Bombs used in WWII). According to the newsletter my uncle had worked at "the Hoover Corporation and was granted several patents." He was also "a successful real estate developer and made his fortune in the post-war housing boom and stock market."[7]

---

[7] http://www.physics.umn.edu/alumni/Newsletter7.pdf

All of the Above

Another thing about equality is that it cannot co-exist with rape...And it cannot co-exist with pornography or with prostitution or with the economic degradation of women on any level, in any way...because implicit in all those things is the inferiority of women.

–Andrea Dworkin

Obsession is the thread that knots me together, my stranglehold of survival. I often ask myself, is having numerous obsessions the same as having one grandiose addiction? I like to think of myself as eclectic, passionately loving sex, and wine, and cigarettes, and slot machines, and shopping at thrift stores. I don't like the word addiction.

I hold Mother responsible for the gambling. I remember when casinos first opened in Minnesota, when slot machines took nickels and quarters. By then mother was in a wheelchair, and touting a supply of oxygen, so it was cumbersome to take her to garage sales on weekends. Instead, I or one of my siblings, would pick her up at her assisted living building, maneuver her heavy wheel chair into the trunk of our car, and drive her to the casino where she became a senior citizen on a mission, throwing nickels and quarters into her favorite machine, not so politely pushing her wheel chair into someone who might have gotten to her favorite machine before her.

Back then, I watched Mother gamble more than I played, and because mother had a curfew I didn't stay all hours of the night, as I sometimes do now. Sometimes, as I watch money disappear I curse Mother, but more often than not I pray to her, "send me a big win, Mother, now." Sometimes she answers, but more likely than not, she's in heaven playing a slot machine that always pays out the big win she so deserved.

I tell myself the casino is the only place a woman without a partner can go by herself, alone but not, surrounded by throngs of people and noise. I tell myself I go to the casino because it is the only place I can feel comfortable smoking because there is so much smoke, even in the non-smoking sections, that I might as well smoke. I tell myself I'm not spending money I don't have to spend. I tell myself there's nothing I need to buy, so why not spend money entertaining myself at a slot machine. I tell myself my sisters like to gamble; if I want to hang out with my sisters I might as well go to the casinos with them.

My sister often wants to go to a casino for the buffet, and I go along with her—I do love to eat! *If it's not harmful to others, it's okay*, my sister told me.

I tell myself shopping at garage sales and thrift stores is a smart way to shop, but I buy things I don't need, don't wear, don't use, but, hey, I recycle. And even though I sometimes find bargains for $1.49, more often than not I leave the Goodwill having spent $25—which adds up when generally a week doesn't go by without shopping! And even though I find *Blanque* shirts and *The Big Shirt* by Carole Tomkins, or artists' hand woven vests, *or J-41* or *Munro*, or *Privo* shoes, I have no place to wear them except to a casino where most of the gamblers are dressed in blue jeans and t-shirts and tennis shoes, and usually so am I.

And, what about ALCOHOL, in capital letters? Name the writers who were drunks—Charles Bukowski at the top of my list. Do we write better in an inebriated state? I don't know. I don't drink and write; I don't write drunk. But, I've been drunk, more than once, and several times I've blacked out.

I wonder if my gambling father, he played Mahjong with the Chinese men at work, and bet on the horses at Canterbury Park, was a drunk? I don't know. (Maybe tending bar for many years motivated him not to drink.) Gambling and drinking can go hand in hand; but, sometimes gamblers are alcoholics who have given up one addiction for another. Rumor has it my grandfather on my mother's side was a gambler and an alcoholic, but I don't know if that was true either. My mother didn't drink, although I want to imagine the *Tom and Jerrys* she mixed at Christmas had a dash of brandy in them! Were they really non-alcoholic? She did add whiskey to our string bean chop suey.

My mother had no overwhelming compulsions, except to keep her daughters safe (Mother used to say if I was going out and planned to drink alcohol, I should eat beans first), even if that meant lying to them and teaching them to be afraid. What does it mean to keep our daughters safe?

Late 1960s: I might have graduated from college in less than twenty years if I had started out at a community college with fewer students and a smaller campus—less overwhelming, easier to get involved. Although, after the U of M, I attended Minneapolis Community College, but I was only there for one-and-a-half terms because life got in the way. I was co-editor of the newspaper, on student council, made friends, liked the teachers. I hung out with a girl I met who was active in school and outside activities. I joined her co-ed bowling team. I thought this one guy liked me; we hung out together. One night he invited me to his apartment. I was gang raped. First one guy, then another. The third guy was reluctant, a virgin. They bullied him. Shame. He belonged to a fraternity, maybe they all did. He later asked me to go to a fraternity party with him, and I did. Closure. That's the last I remember. But, it wasn't the last time in my life I would be raped.

Early 1970s: My boss, at the manufacturing company I worked at, and I had become friends. I often talked about how he had been discriminated as a Jew, and I talked about how I had been discriminated as a Chinese Black woman. One afternoon, as I was about to take the long bus ride home to my husband and children, he asked me to come into his office. He pulled down his pants and tried to jam his penis in my mouth. The next day my husband went to the office and told him I wouldn't be coming back and demanded severance pay, which I received. Years later, by my invitation, in a fit of loneliness and self-pity, the man got from me what he had wanted. Closure.

Late 1970s: I was secretary to the vice president of a small company. My job included planning an intimate party for him and the woman he was having an affair with. When my boss was on vacation with his wife, I was to appease his mistress. Once my boss was in flight with his wife, I took the envelope he had given me, which contained his freshly plucked pubic hairs, and mailed it to his mistress. However, one mistress wasn't enough. I was asked to write a personals ad for my boss (and one for me). I went along with my job duties—until one day I asked for some real work. I didn't know enough to sue for harassment, nor could I afford a lawyer, but I did what I did best—I wrote a letter to my boss' boss, with several cc's. The next day, my boss didn't come to work. Instead, the Marketing Manager came to my office and suggested I quit. My unemployment application was approved. Closure.

Early 1980s: I was an office manager for a fireplace insert distributor. I had gone in to work on a Saturday. A warehouse worker was working in the warehouse. He asked me to come see something in the warehouse. In the warehouse he tried to seduce me. When I said no he got viciously aggressive. I screamed and yelled and told him to get the hell away from me, from the warehouse, from the office—and he fled. I left a note for my boss explaining what had happened and said I wouldn't be back. Monday morning the boss called me. To my surprise, the warehouse man had been fired, and I was asked to come back to work. Closure.

Late 1980s. At a party I was drunk, so I went to a room to sleep it off before driving home. Two men raped me. I clearly remember saying *no*, as I drifted off into nether land, but knew when I regained consciousness that not only one (the one still in bed with me), but two men had raped me; one who I knew, the other a stranger. I must have blacked out.

I was afraid to tell my boyfriend what happened, but I did. And that was the end of boyfriend. He was angry because he was home watching my sons while I was being raped. Closure.

I went to a non-labeling nonprofit support group to find out if I was an

alcoholic and if it was my fault I had been raped. *Shame.* Is it true that we are responsible for all things that happen to us, even the bad things? If a plane crashes, do we choose to be on that plane? If I drank too much scotch, did I choose to be raped? After a brief conversation, the counselor assured me I was not an alcoholic, thank my lucky stars, but when I drank I drank too much too fast and my small body couldn't handle it.

I still drink, occasionally, but (mostly) in moderation, and (mostly) red wine which has antioxidants.

Years ago, when my brother returned home from living temporarily in Arizona, he brought with him stories of skinheads with guns and being followed. The inquiring soul that I was prompted me to ask my brother if I could interview him about his past alcohol and drug use. (I had been his support buddy years before when he went through treatment. I was asked to write a letter regarding my relationship with my brother, especially in regard to drinking. Group leader response was that I was also an alcoholic. I handed my brother my Bible and deserted him. I'm not sure he's ever forgiven me.)

We sat for hours, drinking beer as I asked questions and he answered them. I was particularly interested in stories concerning kin, wondering if any one of us were to blame for influencing another, and wondering how, or if, our various obsessions/addictions were related. Do we have a genetic propensity towards addiction or are social/historical factors the culprit, factors that lead to low self-esteem that lead to obsessive behaviors? My brother told me he had once approached our dad at Dad's work, and our dad denied knowing who he was; he denied that his son was his son!

> **Do you think the reason you use drugs is because addictions are inherited?**
> I don't believe it's because someone in my family may have had a problem . . . . It's how I grew up—the environment I grew up in. It's not fate—if you really want to quit it's your choice.
>
> –interview with my brother

Both of my sons have had DUI's (driving under the influence). Perhaps I spent too much time trying to protect them like my mother tried to protect me (however, I was vocal, my mother silent) to notice when the drinking began.

Once, a few blocks from home, my son, having just gotten his driver's license, was stopped by police. The police followed him to our backyard driveway. My son's brother was in the back seat of the police car. My son and a few of his friends were still sitting in my son's car. I ran out to see what was going on. The policeman said that kids from the city were stealing cars from the suburbs. He thought my son had stolen the car. He hadn't. It was his car. Did several colorful teenage boys equal theft? I spent hours on the phone seeking justice—an apology, something, but to no avail.

Was I so race-absorbed that I didn't know my sons were drinking in high school?

How does a mother, especially knowing her own drinking behavior, not have empathy for her sons that abuse alcohol? And how does she untangle how two brothers went up against each other, alcohol being the substance that fueled the fire, but not the trigger that shot the gun. According to Michael:

> It was guys' weekend at their father's cabin. Everyone had been drinking. David had brought a friend, the friend used the "N" word—over and over and over again throughout the day. By that evening, Michael had had enough. An argument ensued. Next morning Michael apologized—for what? For speaking up? Dave did not defend his brother, despite the fact that one of the reasons he dropped out of college was that his roommates had a habit of making racist remarks. That's how it began.

> It ended with the father and David and his friend returning home the next morning, leaving Mike alone and hung over. Mike went to a neighbor's cabin and drank with that neighbor. Then, despite warnings not to, Mike broke into his father's cabin to sleep off another day of drinking.

> Awakened by the policeman who was called by the father who was called by a next-door neighbor (not the one Mike had been drinking with earlier), who told the father that Mike had broken into the cabin—Mike was arrested. Mike's father had called the police hoping Mike would have to go to treatment. Mike spent the night in jail. The next day he walked seventeen miles, in broken flip flops, back to the cabin, back to his car.

> Months later, Mike was slapped on the hand, told to attend an AA meeting or two, and that was that.

Except, Michael did not stop drinking. A few years later I tried intervention. I was surprised by the initial support of his father, his stepfather, his stepmother, his wife's family, his brother, and his brother's partner, but when it came time to intervene, I was on my own.

Not giving up, I proceeded with an online intervention (seriously, who would do such a thing). I told Michael in an email how much I loved him, how much I wanted him to get help, and how to get the help I thought he needed. After I sent the email, I called him.

My son said, in a sincere and respectful way, thanks, but no thanks.

How many times has he been kicked out of bars? How many times has his wife or my brother gone to pick him up? We all know when Michael is drunk because whenever he is drunk he calls everyone he knows. I know that calling out. I have been calling out most of my life. We all imagine love in different ways, and we all search endlessly for it—especially self-love.

I wonder if Michael has ever forgiven me for the night I called him and his wife to pick me up at the home I was living in with my college sweetheart, reunited after forty some years. (I always believed he was slumming when he dated me back in college, yet still today he believes how we are so much alike, thinking his white life growing up in Southwest Minneapolis with a mother raising three children while his dad went to law school, was the same as me a Black Chinese girl passing for white in South Minneapolis, growing up with a mother who raised five children on welfare.)

I was upset because my boyfriend, although he had gone to bankruptcy court with me that day, couldn't take the time he promised me to go to lunch afterwards and debrief (really, an hour for lunch, what was so important that he had to cancel lunch?).

It was an emotionally difficult time for me. So, I asked his friend if she would meet me. I met her at a bar where we each had a couple of Merlots; mine were on an empty stomach. She then suggested buying a bottle of wine and going back to her house where I admittedly drank too much and still hadn't eaten, except for the ice cream and cake her son surprised me with because he knew the next day was my birthday.

When I had returned home the door was locked and I didn't have a key. When finally my partner opened the door, he told me I couldn't stay. He called the police. It was his house, though all my belongings were there because we had been living together for six months. I took what I could. He refused to give me the $900 mattress I bought to replace his thirty-year- old mattress (not that it would have fit in my car).

That night my son came to get me. The next day I went to work in the clothes I had slept in on the couch at my son's apartment, and taught school that night in those same clothes. It was my birthday. The boyfriend, who had called the police and told me to take all my belongings, called and said I would really like my birthday present. The present wasn't another dead pheasant or five dollar size ten mood ring; it was an original copy of a chapbook I had been searching for to no avail, *Tribes* by Martha Courtot. I met him when my class was over; we are still friends.

How many times might my sons have seen me drunk?

CONSTIPATION *Beauty and the Beast(s)*

"Minnesota lays claim to 51 KKK chapters active during 1920-1930."

Elizabeth Dorsey Hatle

My body has always been a time bomb ready to explode, built of stories my mother never told me of Ku Klux Klan and lynchings, race riots, segregation, civil rights sit-ins and marches—and rapes (although she did tell me not to walk in front of the shoe repair shop on the way from junior high school because the ol' man that owned it liked to stand in the window exposing himself to young girls).

I have been constipated all of my life. As a child, I was afraid of bathrooms. Mother chastised me for reaching up to use a hand towel in a public restroom at Minnehaha Falls; it wasn't sanitary. When I was older, I held my pee because entering a bathroom would, more likely than not, mean seeing myself in a mirror and I didn't want to see my ugly reflection.

Beauty is the mythical standard, like the concept of race that has socialized me to believe there is a universal truth that I am "other" and I must strive to assimilate. For my mother, assimilation was "hiding," for my father assimilation was jumping in the pot and melting. For me, assimilation has been a determination to stand out to fit in—an uneasy camouflage.

Often I was constipated. For me, every other week or two or three was regular, and often preceded by sharp pains down my leg, nausea, and sometimes vomiting. Once I ended up in the emergency room of a hospital because I had debilitating stomach pains. The doctor showed me the x-ray. I was full of crap.

History has a way of imprisoning us until we learn it, until we know it and we know that it will always be part of who we are, but it doesn't have to annihilate us. Recently my bowel movements became every other day or two or three occurrences. What had changed? I sometimes still had pain in my lower right side, a sign, I suppose, not to let up my guard, not to think I had reached some sort of enlightenment, not to forget a grueling history of Black people, Asian people, of Mixed-Race people in America.

Perhaps my recent body function changes have something to do with the fact I was laid off from my job and no longer had to wear corporate shoes that pinched (or the fact I started taking probiotics).

For several years our unit hosted a Halloween party. I spent days, weeks, and the night before the first year's party anxiety stricken as to what to wear. I almost didn't go to work that day. Why had it been so difficult to put on a disguise? I had been wearing a variety of masks all my life. The next year's party I dressed as a trauma drama queen! In my high heels and sequined gown and bright red hair, I almost felt like myself.

Often I tried to explain to anyone at work that would listen that diversity needed to be more than a few designated events per year (Black History Month, Asian Pacific American Heritage Month, American Indian Heritage Month). I was our unit's self-proclaimed diversity guru. It got tiring. I too often was angry. I let it slide. There were too few of us who wanted to create change, and a few of the few who had been employed at the company the longest knew too well change was never going to happen.

Sometimes we have to let go of hope in order to breathe.

Nomad No More

I am a sixty-four year old single woman with a low/average income, student loans in forbearance, and a bankruptcy on my credit report; however, I was able to buy a home. Foolish, naïve, determined—and lucky, I now live in a new neighborhood with a new perspective on taking control of my life.

Nomad. For forty-seven years, since I left my childhood home at the age of nineteen, I have lived in more than fifty different homes (and held more than fifty different jobs), in five different states. I moved because I had to. I moved because I wanted to. I moved because someone else wanted me to. I moved for love. I moved to get away from love. I moved because the moon was full and I was foolhardy. My most recent move, moved me, surprised me, challenged my bravado. Told me some things are not true, some things are.

I had no money and not the best credit, but I was paying $720 for rent in an unkempt, noisy apartment building with no heat or too much heat, broken windows, mold, and any number of annoying problems. I had been feeling sorry for myself for being such a loser: no partner, no home, no career, and no extra dollars. I would forgo the penthouse, exercise rooms, stainless steel appliances, and a short commute to work for anything that came with a mortgage.

However, I didn't plan to take advantage of low interest rates and foreclosed homes. My plan was to take control of my life. Stop whining about relationships, renting, winter—any number of, perhaps unrelated, things. It was time, I thought, to plan my future.

An ad for a senior high rise, enticed me. There was something seductive about the neighborhood and about the building itself. It's subtle curve. How it leaned into the sky. How the price was—affordable. However, by the time I was pre-approved for a loan, the affordable unit was sold. Other units in the building I couldn't afford, especially the remodeled unit with a tenth floor view of star filled nights.

The story I am trying to avoid is reminiscent of too many stories. The roommate who locked me out of our apartment when I told her I was Black. The apartment that was suddenly unavailable when I showed up in person. The all white neighborhood I grew up in. The Lutheran church I was a member of that said no Black people were welcome. And now, full circle, the senior high rise I wanted to live in—well all the seniors I saw who lived in that building, well they all reminded me of the Swedes and Norwegians that had dominated Our Redeemer Lutheran Church.

~ ~ ~

Dear xxxx,
Congratulations on purchasing a new home. I know you are thrilled that you are buying a nice house for a very low price in North Minneapolis. I know you are happy that you'll get to live in a diverse neighborhood. I know, because you told me, the North Side community welcomes you, a white girl from rural Iowa.

§

I found a realtor on the World Wide Web. He recommended a mortgage broker: *if anyone can get you a mortgage, this man could*. I was pre-approved— for less than some people pay for cars, although I had a bankruptcy on my record, my student loan was in forbearance, and I had no savings account— my credit was teetering on good. Tears of joy. I was going to own a home.

§

I also know why your happiness makes me angry. As a white person you can use your unearned privilege to move anywhere you want and expect to be safe, and even welcome without giving it any or much thought.

§

WAS I REALLY WORRIED ABOUT HOW NEIGHBORS WOULD REACT TO ME, OR WAS I WORRIED ABOUT HOW I WOULD REACT TO THEM?

§

When I was a kid one of my mother's sisters lived in North Minneapolis with her children, in the projects—how much choice did she have? Another aunt moved into the, then, Jewish neighborhood in North Minneapolis—was she, a Black woman with a Black husband and several Black children safe or welcomed?

§

Silly me. I hadn't thought about the down payment or other expenses. I can't believe I asked Ex Husband Number Four to loan me the down payment, but asking is what we sometimes have to do to take control of our lives. Ex Husband Number Four *gifted* me the down payment.

§

Yes, that was a long time ago, but don't fool yourself into thinking racism has disappeared. Just the other day in Minneapolis three Black men were stabbed because the white man that stabbed them didn't like Black people. Just the other day, I saw KKK painted in large letters across a garage in a Minneapolis suburb.

§

I earned extra expense money from a teaching job. The bottom line isn't always the bottom line. There are half truths and avoidances. Extra expenses included an inspection and fees and interest I only half understood. And boxes and bubble wrap and movers. And locks and window coverings and cleaning supplies. And painters: $10/hour—and pizza and beer.

§

The process of finding a home, putting in an offer, and closing took three months. My realtor, mortgage broker, and closer were patient and mostly calm—unlike me, the frustrated, impatient, nervous, sometimes angry buyer. I was in control of some things: checking the MLS listings daily, telling the realtor which townhomes I wanted to see, and waiting to hear which ones I couldn't see because they weren't FHA approved. Most things I had no control over: where properties I could afford were located and the condition of the properties I could afford.

§

When I found a home I could afford in a neighborhood I wasn't familiar with, I asked myself who lives here—any people of color, any GLBT, any writers, any activists, any grandmothers, any . . . . With no time for answers, I wrote an offer which was accepted. I kept telling myself, if they don't like me it's their problem. If they don't like me, it's their problem. I kept telling myself I was not afraid.

§

I am writing this letter to be honest with you about my feelings. I, too, recently moved. It was never not on my mind if I would be welcome in my new community, and if I would be safe.

§

Both the realtor and the inspector were surprised by the condition of the foreclosed condo I purchased. It was not trashed. The appliances weren't missing. The walls weren't bashed in. Although the property sat empty for a year, there were few cobwebs, no mouse turds, not a stain on the carpet. Okay, there was that smell of dog pee.

§

The townhome I bought is what I could afford. What I could afford wasn't much. No swimming pool, no gym, no balcony, no flowers, no picnic benches. The furnace is twenty-five years old. The dryer doesn't work. The dishwasher is covered with hard water stains. The front door handle is missing. The

Association has no reserves. Next door, another foreclosed property sits empty. However, what isn't much, is much more than I expected—and it's home.

§

These are tough economic times. Tough economic times have allowed me to be a home owner. What irony. I have made one friend where I live. I have made a couple of enemies. Others pay me no mind.

§

And you say you had no other options.

Sincerely,

_____

~ ~ ~

    I now live in Oakdale, Minnesota. The 2000 census said Oakdale is mostly white, but it's not anymore. My friends have visited me—Asian, Mexican, Black, Jewish, white, straight, gay. My cousin has visited; in fact, my cousin's daughter lives next door in Woodbury.

    No one has to visit at night.

    I welcome the next census when I can add one more person of color to a neighborhood that was once mostly white. My friend Lori laughs because she remembers being the only Black student, well she and her siblings, at Tartan High School, just down the street from where I now live. She says where I live used to be farmland.

Fractions

Whites in the United States need some help envisioning the American black experience with ancestral fractions. At the beginning of miscegenation between two populations presumed to be racially pure, quadroons appear in the second generation of continuing mixing with whites, and octoroons in the third. A quadroon is one-fourth African black and thus easily classed as black in the United States, yet three of this person's four grandparents are white. An octoroon has seven white great-grandparents out of eight and usually looks white or almost so. Most parents of black American children in recent decades have themselves been racially mixed, but often the fractions get complicated because the earlier details of the mixing were obscured generations ago. Like so many white Americans, black people are forced to speculate about some of the fractions—one-eighth this, three-sixteenths that, and so on....

F. James Davis, *Who is Black? One Nation's Definition* (1991)

PERSONAL DESCRIPTION

453. *Column 10. Color or Race.*-Write "W" for white; "Neg" for Negro; "In" for Indian; "Chi" for Chinese; "Jp" for Japanese; "Fil" for Filipino; "Hi" for Hindu; and "Kor" for Korean. For a person of any other race, write the race in full.

454. *Mexicans.*-Mexicans are to be regarded as white unless definitely of Indian or other nonwhite race.

455. *Negroes.*-A person of mixed white and Negro blood should be returned as Negro, no matter how small a percentage of Negro blood. Both black and mulatto persons are to be returned as Negroes, without distinction. A person of mixed Indian and Negro blood should be returned as a Negro, unless the Indian blood very definitely predominates and he is universally accepted in the community as an Indian.

456. *Indians.*-A person of mixed white and Indian blood should be returned as an Indian, if enrolled on an Indian agency or reservation roll, or if not so enrolled, if the proportion of Indian blood is one-fourth or more, or if the person is regarded as an Indian in the community where he lives.

457. *Mixed Races.*-Any mixture of white and nonwhite should be reported according to the nonwhite parent. Mixtures of nonwhite races should be reported according to the race of the father, except that Negro-Indian should be reported as Negro.–1940 Census: Instructions to Enumerators

Aunt Grace

2012 census statistics claim 2.2% of Minnesotans are of more than one race.[8]

Aunt Grace wrote "The Plight of the Racial Mixtures," sometime after 1959 when Adam Clayton Powell said to Mike Wallace that 28 million white people have black blood and seventy percent of Negros or 11 million have white blood. It begins:

> Most everyone is familiar with the expression, 'neither flesh, nor fowl, nor good red herring.' This is to a large extent the plight of the American racial mixture, who may be a combination of black and white, red and yellow races and with a complex and varied nationality background. ...

---

[8] http://quickfacts.census.gov/qfd/states/27000.html

For example I am approximately of 1/12 Black African descent and my children are about 1/20. They are also Blackfoot Indian, Irish, English and Norwegian.

My aunt's daughter participated in a workshop I taught, and in the subsequent book that was published, *Chromosomes and Genes* (Guild Press, 1982) she wrote, "My mother's descent is Wyandotte, Blackfoot, and some Black." In that same book I wrote, "My mother is Irish, Indian, and African American (as far as I know)."

I have never been good at math, however, if my aunt is 1/12 Black, how is my cousin 1/20 Black? My aunt is my mom's sister. If she is only 1/12 Black and not 100% then I would not be ½ Black, but only 1/24 Black and my children wouldn't be ¼ Black, they would only be 1/48 Black. And, Indian?

I know that my great grandma was brown-skinned and her daughter, my grandmother, was ½ white having been conceived by the plantation owner's Irish son. And I know that my grandfather was white and his mother Black (I don't know about my great grandfather on my grandfather's side of the family). So then, not going back any further which gets complicated, grandma and grandpa would both be half Black and half white, wouldn't they? And if they are half Black and half white, my mom would be ½ Black and ½ white and I would be ¼ Black, ¼ white—and ½ Chinese.

At some point I came to terms with the fact I am Chinese and Negro because that's what my birth certificate says and it made my life less complicated. But when I discovered what my aunt and my cousin claimed to be their racial background, I was bewildered. I began to think was I Black at all? What is the size of a drop? Why did my mom make such a deal of "passing" if she wasn't't/we weren't Black? Why have I spent my life writing about my racial identity over "a drop" and why do I think race has anything to do with my children when the "drop" hardly even exists for them?

It has been said if you write enough about a subject, you will make sense of it. I have written so much about being Black/Chinese passing for white that recently I thought, *am I white*? I was raised white—raised in a white neighborhood, went to a white church, went to school with white children. Why would I think that I wasn't white? Why would I not want to be white?

Memory is emotion. Memory lives in my body, wrinkles my brow, and slits my tongue. Memory cradles sorrow and longing. I know more than I know. Wisdom is a cramp in my leg and I can't stand up to shake it loose. Memory has me by the gray hairs on my head. I can't bleach it white or mask it with the color black.

Flashback: My sister is ten months older than me. Mother said she didn't have sex with my father after my sister was born. Am I a virgin birth?

According to a former teacher, virgin births happen as often as twins. If I am a virgin birth, am I Chinese?

Present Tense

It is not always the absence of love
That makes me seem alone.
Often it's been too much love
Given to me by the wrong people
For the wrong reasons
That keeps me here,
Gladly alone,
Rather than have the life sucked
Out of me by the violent needs
Of other minds and bodies. . . .

from *My Song for Him Who Never Sang to Me,*
by Merrit Malloy

Okay, I am judgmental, I admit it. My one fault, my dark side, my worst enemy. Give me an excuse to condemn you and I will. Tear you down, cut out your heart, spew venom—make you want to hate me, make you want to leave me (make you want me to leave). Usually it works.

Sometimes he loves me forever, dreams of me coming back as he ejaculates to my photo, the one he made a copy of to keep.

It's my defense mechanism, my running away without being the one to run. It's his/her fault; I let them take the fall. I have to be right, be righteous. Otherwise I'd be wrong and history be damned.

Otherwise my mother passed for white to protect me for no reason, otherwise my birth certificate documenting mother's race Negro, father's race Chinese is a sham, otherwise my mom and dad would still be married, otherwise I would still be married (to the first ex husband or the second, or the third, or the fourth), otherwise my son wouldn't have had everything Black associated with him beginning at the age of three, otherwise there would have been no family secrets, otherwise I wouldn't be writing this book.

I won't let you be right because then I would have to be wrong and the only thing I have that is mine, that is real, is what I believe to be true. I hang on to my truths as a matter of life and death.

I am sitting in a hotel room, a casino hotel, The Grand Casino, in Hinckley Minnesota. I have five nights free; why not take advantage of a desk that doesn't belong to me. Away from my own 800 square foot condo where there are always meals to cook, dishes do wash, clothes to put away—all kinds of things to distract me. But nothing is free and I am already out of control. I have gone to the cash machine twice. I ate a hot dog (the cheapest meat on the menu). I played slots, I dreamed of a big win. Almost down to my last dollar, I still had faith my losses would be returned. But no, and it's only the first night, the first six hours. I have already lost $200.

I have a book to write, stories to tell. Writing is my work. I want my writing to make sense of my life. I want my life to have meaning. I want to be in control of my life, at least in control of the things that I should be able to control. I'm not.

I'm always surprised at how other people see me. Confident. Smart. Sassy. Youthful. Truthful. I'm not.

I am sitting in the restaurant of the casino, alone, enjoying my meal. Across from me is a tall elegant Black man with his white wife, and mixed-race daughter. The daughter is beautiful. The father is handsome. The wife is not the Barbie doll woman people rant about. She is obese, plain Jane, the one I think I am better than. I think *why not me instead of the white woman, why not me the mixed-race child desiring the love of a Black man, desiring an intimate embrace of my family's history I was told to hide, an intimate window into who I am?* But no, I am fortunate if a white man finds me attractive.

I see older white couples and think I am glad it's not me with the man with a beer belly sitting across from the wife in silence. You see the couples' resignation; you see boredom, as they lift their fork to their mouth, food the only thing that sustains them. Of course this is a lie. I will take whoever will have me. My belly is not the flat shape it once was. Desire is gone, be gone.

But, if you think you love me, make sure you have a pliable heart, sympathy and compassion. Most of all, you must be vulnerable and non-defensive. You must read my mind, read my books. You must be the missionary on the bottom accepting what I have to give, knowing what you think I need and what you are willing to give may be different than what I want or need.

Although, truthfully, I don't always want to be on top while you lay there unaccountable; yet, I often feel suffocated when the heavy weight of you is upon me. Truthfully, I want you to want me enough to initiate once in a while. I want your needs to be as great as mine.

Damn it. I want this relationship to work. It won't.

I am not Cinderella. You are not Prince Charming. It's not a fairy tale. The ending is unimaginable, though it usually ends like this: I run away. I find home in self-pity and self-destruction. I may or may not have hurt your feelings.

DAY TWO: It is 10 a.m. Finally, the chill is out of the air and I feel rested. I slept in the pink, black, and gray sweater with the Scandinavian design to keep me warm. I will not change my clothes, take a shower or eat breakfast. I have my *Herbal Slimming Tea* and that is enough sustenance for now. It will help me poop, and get rid of the shit that's been accumulating.

I went to bed after an intense Google search relating to the history of racism in Minnesota and discovered Duluth, MN, just an hour from Hinckley, MN where I am staying, is in the news. The "Un-fair" Campaign that had been brewing for about a year, incensed skinheads enough to protest outside the government center. One of the billboards stated: It's hard to see racism when you're white. One poster stated: Is white skin really fair skin?

In 1920 three traveling circus workers were lynched in Duluth, Minnesota—Elias Clayton, Elmer Jackson, and Isaac McGhie. They were accused, along with several other circus workers, of raping a white woman, but there was no medical evidence. The site of the lynchings is where a casino now stands.

I realize it is where memory and current experience (whether mine or someone else's) collide that necessitates that I write my story.

I DON'T UNDERSTAND, he says

> *The pre-Adamite view* argues that blacks, particularly so-called "Negroes," are not descended from Adam. ...
>
> These writers (all of them white), argued that blacks belong to a race created before Adam and from among whom the biblical villain Cain found his wife. Cain, by marrying one of these pre-Adamic peoples, the reasoning goes, became the progenitor of all black people. Therefore, it was rationalized, black people, especially "Negroes," are not actually human, because they did not descend from Adam but from some pre-Adamic creation, having entered the human race only by intermarriage, and that with a notorious sinner. As non-humans, therefore, they did not have souls, but were merely beasts like any other beast of the field. And since the Bible says God gave humans dominion over the beasts, it was concluded that these soulless creatures exist to do work for the humans.
>
> This preposterous theological premise was preached in churches across the United States, particularly in the Southeast, to reassure people that slavery was not only acceptable, but the very will of God, rooted firmly in a "proper" understanding of the Bible
>
> –Dr. Dan Rogers[9]

Cinderella wants a prince! No wonder she has so many pairs of shoes. It's about love, but she can only imagine it. Why? She's kissed too many frogs.

The recipe is simple. Mix what I didn't know with what I now know. Mix the history, not only of where I live, in the state of Minnesota, but national and world history, take it back to biblical times, take it back to the beginning of time, take it back and mix it with what I do know—my mother's relatives could only visit at night when it was dark and the neighbors couldn't see them and most importantly, we couldn't see ourselves! Mix and stir and agitate. Add

---

[9] http://www.gci.org/bible/white

tears and sweat and chills and fever. Add secrets and denial. Add relatives in China. Unknown relatives. Cousins on my mother's family side who are also "mixed-up"—add jealousy and desire. Add my dead mother and my dead father. Add divorce. Add drinking. Add gambling. Add shopping. Add sex. Cook until done, burn it to a crisp, but savor it anyway. Taste each bite, each emotion, and each dysfunction. Chew on the anger, the madness, and the truth. Never free from the ashes, from the fallout, from the longing. Never free from the longing for love.

What is it I imagine? What is love? Why do I think I've never experienced it? Why do I think I have always given it so freely? Why do I think I never have gotten it back? Love can't be I didn't do it. I wasn't even born. My best friend's sister's husband is Black. We are all God's children. Oh, but you're different.

Love is action, not just words. Go to the library, read a book about racism, about oppression. Read my books. Don't feel sorry for me. Don't take the missionary position. You're probably too fat anyway with the lies you tell your white and privileged self. The economy is changing. Some of you will know recession. Some of you will experience a loss of power. Some of you will never be on top again, but still behave like you are, because you can.

However, when you lie beneath me, too fat to straddle my blithe and beautiful body, cocky in your position, too blind to see you are on the bottom, to see we have changed positions know that I know more tricks than you will ever know. I will jam you with every racist sexist injury done to myself and others. You like that I am crying. You think I am crying because I am satisfied. I'm not.

Maybe for you it's orgasmic. For me it's organic. A natural release of pent up anger. Sixty-four years old, but still, I can outlast you. Even on the bottom, you tire quickly. I don't want to stop. You fall asleep.

Ignorance is bliss. You will never know it's not love. Thus, you will never need to imagine what love is.

Cinderella has tried on too many shoes. Some too small, some too large, some too fancy, some too plain. She is crazy, that Cinderella. Never knows what she wants, what she likes. One day the red high heels, the next it's brown penny loafers. Some shoes she lets hang around in her closet for years, others she recycles on a whim. The problem with Cinderella, she is more complicated than the fairy tales make her out to be. She's not Cinderella, she's Snow White; she's not Snow White, she's Prince Charming; she's not Prince Charming, she's *frog*.

"What would you do if you had been in my shoes?"
"I don't understand," he says, I would never have been in your shoes."
"But imagine if you were."

"I can't," he says.

One doesn't have to imagine love, if one is love; one doesn't even have to know why one might be love—there is no need to yearn for wisdom. But, one might be pissed off and might even cry when one realizes I am not love, that I can only imagine it, can only fake it because it isn't really the prince that I want, what I want is intangible; I may never be able to put my words around it.

Life After Death

For a century, it was standard practice at many American insurance companies: When it came to burial insurance, blacks were charged more than whites for the same coverage...

That racial bias was built into these policies was long an open secret in the insurance industry. Insurance forms asked the applicant's race, and black were routinely charged more than whites for the same coverage, the insurance industry now publicly acknowledges...

Typically, it was one third more, according to lawyers representing black policy holders...

In many cases, industry critics say, premiums paid over the years greatly exceeded the payout value of the policies.

Article printed in Quad City Times (AP)

After my mother died of a leukemia blast, April 1999, her dream unfulfilled of wanting to see the new millennium and the supposed end of the world, my sister said, but *Mother never said she loved us*. Awkwardly, I said, "really." I tried to explain that my need to have Mother love me was reconciled for me years earlier, in my thirties. A woman, my elder, and classmate in community college explained to me that *my mother would never love me the way I wanted her to love me*. A simple, yet bold statement that eased my anxiety, and allowed me to move forward. Mother did love me, she just couldn't say it. She did love me, but I must have been a painful reminder, like looking in a mirror; seeing me must have reminded her of who she was—a Black woman, passing for white, once married to a Chinese man.

One day, Mother and I sat in her low income high rise, at a table full of prescription drugs, hair curlers, jelly beans, and mail. She had agreed to share some of her stories. However, we barely had begun our conversation when the tape recorder quit working and simultaneously my mother said she couldn't go on with what must have felt like an interrogation. To me, that was a signal, a

Sarah Ella Franklin Quan (1913 - 1999)

sign that I was not to know the secrets buried in my mother's heart. I asked her if she couldn't go on because she is Black or because she has always been poor. *Shame.* A little of both was her reply.

I accepted then that my mother and I would never truly understand each other, although maybe the truth is we understood each other more than we could bear to admit. I continued to bring my mother gifts of Hershey Kisses and trashy newspapers. More often than not, I hugged her, best as I could, as she sat in her wheel chair, an oxygen tube to her nose, and I kissed her on the forehead and said "I love you."

Once she replied, in almost a whisper, "you know We are proud of you." I knew that was her way of saying she loved me in the only way she could. I imagine how it must have grieved her when my writing exposed family secrets that she would rather have kept buried. Yet, I think in some small way she loved me for my courage to say and be what she as a mother could not because of what she knew and experienced as a Black woman growing up during the depression, and World War II—and raising five children during the civil rights era.

My siblings and I gathered around Mom's hospital bed, the day that was to be our last of many hospital visits that occurred over several years. I watched as the bruises on her body became darker and larger and more prevalent. I watched her die from a leukemia blast, the one thing the doctor said she wouldn't die of. I thought it would be her heart.

I watched and observed her transcending her years of secrets and silence and saw a light, a white light (how ironic) illuminating her entire being. I said to my brother that mom would die that night. His anger at my pronouncement caused me to retract what I said, and apologize, lying that I didn't know. I asked my sister to call my sister in Arizona and tell her to get on the next plane home. Her response was similar to my brother's, "there's no hurry," she said.

I couldn't get myself to leave my mother's bedside, even after my siblings had gone for the day. I knew what I was waiting for. But mother told me to go home, so finally I left. Fifteen minutes after arriving home, the phone call came, Mother had died. Apparently she wanted to die alone. My sister in Arizona was called and told the news and the rest of us returned to the hospital, waiting.

When my sister arrived from the airport my siblings, my children, and Ex Husband Number Four took up vigil next to our mother, now covered in a white sheet. For me, the aura surrounding Mom was whiter than any whiteness she could ever have imagined herself to be. But it was a translucent light, a light illuminating the beauty of who she was, always the loving, protective mother trying her best to keep her children safe in a world that would always keep them in danger. I loved her more than ever, as she lay dead, no longer weary from having to work so hard to provide for us and to protect us. We, on the other hand, were immobile, waiting in agitated silence. Although crying was inevitable, we would leave the room to cry and then return, our tears brushed away. How long did we stand this way not knowing what to do?

Finally, I blurted out that I had always wanted to be a minister, so if anyone wanted to join hands and pray I would say a few words. And I did. From the Lutheran liturgy that I had at one time cherished, *may the peace of God which passes all understanding, be with you* and some other tip of my tongue holy mutterings. And that was that. I swear that if I hadn't acted, we would still be standing in my mother's hospital room.

Sometime after my mother's death, my sister received an extra check from Mom's "penny" insurance policy. The check was repayment of overpayments due to the fact that Mother is Black. My siblings and I cashed the check, and went to the state fair. No one talked about where the money came from.

Humility

President Barack Obama's campaign slogan, "Yes We Can" was stirring; however, can we?

How many *feel-good-if-you-work-hard-you-can-make-it* success stories have I heard? More than enough! I always cringe when I hear them, especially from politicians. I talk back to the media whether television or print journalism *who are you kidding, it's not an axiom that works for all, there is no fairy tale*. I've worked hard, I've done the work, all the right things, been employed most of my life (went back to work a week after my first child was born), even when laid off from full-time work I made my own work by establishing a recycled clothes business.

I believe in continuing education and continued my education (twenty years to earn an undergraduate degree, two to earn an MFA) despite detours looking for love, marriage, children, and work; and despite low self-esteem—*you can't do it, why do you want to do it*. And, I'm not alone. If hard work is the key to success, there would be a lot more of us successful. Politicians will never admit their rhetoric makes *those that don't have* at blame for their lack of success, *shame*, while they keep hidden from the public that greed is often the reason the poor are poor.

I know I've worked hard and achieved a master's education, still the rhetoric defies me—where is this success that hard work and education was supposed to earn me? I've survived, but *Survival is not enough* my peers tell me, we deserve more.

But I believe, after much remembering, much writing about a Chinese Black girl passing for white, born shortly after WWII, fearful of an atomic bomb and *why didn't we have a bomb shelter*, John F. Kennedy shot, Viet Nam, Martin Luther King, Jr. shot, Jim Crow, KKK—when I think of the history I was born into, and that I've lived through, I believe success for me IS survival. Survival based in humility. Humility is what comes after fear, after anger, after shame, after voice. Humility is my everyday challenge. *Yes I can*, survive.

The fact that I learned to speak, to write, to not bottle up my emotions, but instead communicate, have conversations, write with as much honesty as I could risk, with as much humility as I could muster—this IS my survival, this is my success.

My sister said she wants to know what it is she is supposed to learn in this life. I flippantly answered we're doing what we're supposed to do, answering my own question instead of hers. I don't know if that means I believe in fate, I don't think I do, or at least I believe in responsibility more than fate—I believe in karma; maybe I believe we all do the best we can. Who is to judge what our best is? Who is to say what we can and can't do? I only know that my sister has a generous heart. Her generosity of time and resources has blessed many, especially those in our immediate family. From the time our father disappeared, she, then a sixth grader, took on a major role of caretaking. Her role increased over the years, especially as our mother grew ever more ill in her eighties. When my sister went off to college, I was in sixth grade. She wrote me letters encouraging me to keep writing. (But, I think she meant keep writing my silly little poems!)

One of the reasons it has taken so many years to complete *Love Imagined*, why so many starts and stops, is because honesty makes one vulnerable, can bring on the naysayers, the critics—the biggest critic being myself.

Yes, there are those who don't like my writing, that say I can't write, they didn't teach you how to write in that MFA program you attended—but that criticism is easier to deal with than I hope your life gets better, or writing about racism isn't trendy anymore or writing doesn't save lives!

Because then, as a writer, I question even my own authority over my own life! That's when I question what right do I have to think my story is important? That's when I stop writing. That's when I'm silent. *Shame.* How could I have the audacity to believe that my experiences of racism, sexism, and more recently ageism have anything to do with who I am—and why would anyone care? *Shame.*

How often have I heard white friends say, oh yeah, we ate government food commodities, we were poor, my parents were divorced, I was a single-parent, I've been laid off my job—and I nod my head? Of course you did. But, one can't compare apples to oranges.

A friend remarked, *observing isn't judging.* As a writer I have a responsibility to observe, be objective, not judge, but tell the truth. I am trying not to judge myself.

For me, success isn't measured in financial success, or literary success, or parenting success, or relationship success—it's measured in survival, in making it through another day, humbly thankful and forgiving. Survival is knowing the complexity of who I was, thus who I am, and knowing that I may never come to terms with either. Survival is knowing there may never be someone who truly understands me or accepts me for all of whom I am, even my own siblings, or my children. Survival is knowing I may always be lonely. Survival is knowing I may always be afraid. Yet, survival is also hope, is imagination.

Afterword

> A soulful personality is complicated, multifaceted, and shaped by both pain and pleasure, success and failure. Life lived soulfully is not without its moments of darkness and periods of foolishness.
>
> –Thomas Moore, *Care of the Soul.*

I am sixty-six years old. In 2010, at age sixty-two, I was involuntarily retired from a ten year (minus three months) job three years before I planned to collect Social Security. Months of looking for work, taking classes—*how to write a resume, how to interview, social media, financial management, etc.* brought only disillusionment and despair and financial poverty.

However, I tip-toe between a poverty of and a generosity of spirit. I have always been a seeker of wisdom, but the search has brought an ache of heart so deep it eats me inside and out. However, a generosity of spirit has kept me afloat, pushed me forward, kept me alive—my spirit, my energy, existing through time past and present. As deep and sinister my need for love can be at times, love isn't what I needed. What I needed was acceptance, not yours, mine.

To imagine love is to believe love exists. To imagine love is to see between the lies—the truth that must be written.

I believe in God the Father, Quan Yin, the holy universe—prayer; and, a good night's sleep. I believe in loving.

~ ~ ~

I also believe an ending is a beginning. The ending of a story encourages the beginning of another story. Stories embrace the intellect and emotions of both the writer and the reader. The day before I sent the final manuscript to my editor, a childhood friend read *Love Imagined* and responded with: but my family didn't know! We only knew you were Chinese. How does this change my story? How does this undermine, or not, others who said: but we always knew you were Black? How does it challenge or confirm what I remember or what I think I know?

Stories are living entities. They have lives that outlive the story teller. They are a handshake. They are a slap on the back. They are a heartfelt hug.

My childhood friend, Irish as well as Swedish and Norwegian, whom I've only recently reconnected with, wrote:

Your story was captivating. Your writing style is absolutely beautiful and such a pleasure to read, despite the hard truths. I was often struck by how many emotions and experiences we share, so much so that there were times when I felt you were revealing parts of my life, yet they were intertwined with your deeper story as a woman of mixed-race through the decades of your life. I admire your honesty and courage to speak. No doubt you will help others find their voices or recognize the very personal impact of history on individuals.

–Patricia Holter Ronken

Acknowledgements for Permission to Reprint Previously Published Material

Andrea Dworkin: "I Want a Twenty-Four Hour-Truce During Which There Is No Rape," originally published under the title "Talking to Men About Rape," in *Out!*, Vol. 2, No. 6, April 1984; then under the current title in *M.*, No. 13, Fall 1984. Excerpt reprinted by permission of Elaine Markson, Elaine Markson Literary Agency.

Associated Press: *A century of overcharging blacks, costing insurance industry*. Excerpt reprinted with permission of the Associated Press.

City of Minneapolis: excerpt outlining the Standish Neighborhood, reprinted with permission of the City of Minneapolis.

Robert Coles, in the forward to *Voices from the Whirlwind an Oral History of the Chinese Cultural Revolution by Feng Jicai* –Published by Pantheon, New York, 1991, Fair Use permission granted by Melanie Flaherty, Random House Copyright & Permissions.

Monica Haynes: Excerpt reprinted by permission from the Pittsburgh Post-Gazette.

Leslie Li: Kim Loo Sisters: Portrait in Four-Part Harmony (film), (http://www.leslieli.com/ldl/about.html). Excerpt reprinted by permission of Leslie Li.

J. Llewellyn et al: "The Cold War," Alpha History, accessed Feb. 24, 2014, (http://alphahistory.com/coldwar/). Excerpt reprinted by permission of Manager, Alpha History.

Jeffrey McDonald: http://www.navsource.org/archives/10/16/160951.htm Photo used by permission of Mr. McDonald and Navsource.

Merrit Malloy: *My Song for Him Who Never Sang to Me*, "Wrong Reason" (a Ward Ritchie book, 1975). Excerpt reprinted by permission of Merrit Malloy.

Minnesota Historical Society: "The Chinese American Experience in Minnesota" (http://www.mnhs.org/mhsuse.html). Excerpt reprinted by permission of Pam Videen.

About the Author

Sherry Quan Lee, MFA, Creative Writing is a Community Instructor at Metropolitan State University (Intro to Creative Writing, Advanced Creative Writing), and has taught classes and mentored writers at Intermedia Arts, and the Loft Literary Center; and co-taught *A Gathering of Storytellers* with Lori Young-Williams for the University [of Minnesota] Women of Color organization (UWOC), Urban Research and Outreach-Engagement Center (UROC), a partnership between the University of Minnesota and North Minneapolis, and for other community organizations state wide.

Photo by Charissa Uemura

She is the author of *A Little Mixed Up*, Guild Press, 1982 (second printing), *Chinese Blackbird*, a memoir in verse, published 2002 by the Asian American Renaissance, republished 2008 by Modern History Press, and *How to Write a Suicide Note: serial essays that saved a woman's life*, Modern History Press, 2008.

Follow her online at http://blog.sherryquanlee.com

STUDY GUIDE: things to consider

1. The narrator of *Love Imagined: a mixed race memoir,* imagines love. She expects *love* to acknowledge, understand, and respect the history of and the reality of race, class, gender, sexuality, and age, and how it affects her personally—it hasn't. How do your memories, beliefs, and experiences reflect how you currently define and search for love? Do men and women define and experience love differently?

2. The narrator's mother *passed for white* because she thought it would make her husband feel more comfortable than being married to a Black woman, according to her mother's sister, Grace. However, her husband, apparently, didn't know she was passing. Was she projecting her own experience and fears associated with being Black? What might be some underlying reasons why a person, whose skin color is light enough, in context of American history, would pass for white? In what other contexts do people *pass*?

3. Passing for white created a complicated identity for the narrator. How can one feel good about oneself if one is told they are not good enough to be who they are? But as the narrator increasingly insists on identifying as Chinese and Black, others, literally, don't see her, or choose to ignore her, for who she is. Thus, she is invisible and her lifelong search for love becomes tedious, and heart wrenching. Have you ever felt invisible? How has invisibility impacted who you are?

4. Historically, if a person had one drop of Negro blood, they were classified as Negro. Children conceived of white slave owners and Negro slaves were thus relegated to the, supposedly, lesser identity. Thus, the narrator of *Love Imagined* would be Negro and Chinese as, also, evidenced by her birth certificate, even though her mother was mixed-race. The narrator is actually more Chinese than Black—she is also Irish and Blackfoot Indian.

   The narrator does not like labels, but when forced to identify she has used *biracial, mixed-race, African American, Black, Chinese, Chinese and Black, and Other.* How do you think mixed-race people should identify? What social, political, and cultural implications might impact how mixed-race people choose to identify?

5. What is your reaction when the narrator asks: *Am I merely the white girl I was culturally raised to be?* How does culture affect identity? Consider your culture. How does it affect who you are?

6. The narrator has often run away from people and places in her life. She ran towards love. She ran from love. Although husband number one said *why tell them [his parents] the truth, that you are Black, and not have them like you*, she believed the truth is what mattered. Would you consider her brave or foolish? Have you ever run away? What values were you protecting, or avoiding, if any, by running away?

7. When not running toward or from love, the narrator keeps herself *compulsively* busy. In your opinion, what is the difference between a compulsion and an addiction? Is lack of self-esteem and self-love underlying reasons for compulsive/addictive behaviors?

8. Location is important to the narrator's story. The story begins in *South Scandinavian Minneapolis*, Minnesota and ends in Oakdale, Minnesota. How does identity impact where the narrator has or hasn't lived? Does identity impact where you have lived, or where you are now living?

9. Shame is a recurrent theme in *Love Imagined*, how does the narrator respond to shame? Can you recognize shame? Have you experienced it?

10. The narrator claims she is not a "tragic mulatto." A fairy tale metaphor meanders throughout the memoir, *Love Imagined*. But Cinderella does not live happily ever after with the prince(s), no matter how many pairs of shoes she has. That's not to say she isn't happy. What fairy tales did you grow up with? Would you rewrite them? If so, why? How would you rewrite them based on your personal story? How does one reinvent myth?

11. Despite detours, the narrator achieves a master's education. She worked hard, but never achieved the "success" politicians and others claim she could reach. The narrator believes survival is enough; survival is success. How would you define success? What do you think is needed to achieve it? What do you think hinders achieving success?

12. How do the photographs in *Love Imagined* impact your experience of the story?

Index

M

Madame Butterfly, 14
Malloy, M., 111
marijuana, 46, 51
mediation, 72–73
menstruation, 45–46
Mexicans, 107
MFA, 79–80, 82, 89, 123, 124, 129, 131
middle class, 85
Minnehaha Falls, 99
Mixed-Blood, 51
Moore, T., 125

N

Nankin Café, 14, 15, 22, 50
Negro
    assimilation, 26
    birth certificate, 109
    defined, 107
    denial, 86
    descended from Adam, 115
    mixed-race, 108
    vs. woman, 67
Negro-Indian, 108
nigger, 81, 87
North High School, 3, 5
North Minneapolis, 5, 50

O

Oakdale, MN, 106, 131
one-drop rule, vii, 109, 130
Our Redeemer Lutheran Church, 2, 34, 35, 104

P

passing for white, 3, 5, 9, 26, 72, 85, 97, 109, 119, 123

R

rape, 93–94
Rogers, D., 115
Ronken, P.H, 126

S

Sandvik, J., iv, ix
shame, 34, 38, 42, 58, 59, 62, 79, 131
shoes, 92
    as icons, 7
    Cinderella, 2, 46, 115, 116, 131
    corporate, 100
slaves, i, 56, 130
South Scandinavian Minneapolis, 1–4, 131
Standish, 2, 3, 35, 39
suicide, vi, 65, 80
Suzie Wong, 14

T

Taiwan, 22
tragic mulatto, vi, 131

U

Uemura, C., ix
University of Minnesota, 49, 63, 83, 86, 89, 90, 129

W

West Bank Minneapolis, 46
Wintergreen, 8
World War II, 12, 15, 90, 120, 123

Y

Young-Williams, L., ix, 2, 83

Chinese Blackbird by Sherry Quan Lee

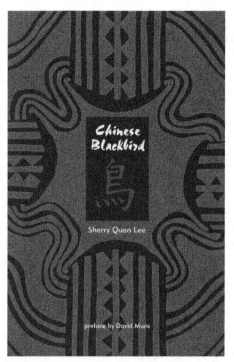

"Quan Lee eloquently expresses how painful and confusing it can be to embrace the many complex identities that one body can contain. With evocative imagery and words that cut straight to the heart, Quan Lee details her lifelong struggles with both the vagaries and concreteness of race, class, gender and sexual identity. Her guilt and shame are palpable. But so too are her emotional and intellectual triumphs. Like a favorite sad song when we have been dumped by the love of our lives, this volume will be oddly comforting to anyone who has ever been overcome by that sorrow which seems insurmountable."

—Eden Torres, Assistant Professor
Women's Studies, Chicano Studies,
University of Minnesota

"It's been a long time since I've been treated to a voice so full of honesty about one's struggle to come to terms with her identity. Through elegant poetry, full of exquisite imagery and detail, Quan Lee takes the reader on her personal, transformative journey in which she explores how race, class, gender and sexual identity inform who she is. Along the way, she encounters rocks and boulders that would have stopped many of us. Instead, she turns them over and examines the creatures hiding in the darkness underneath, leaving no stone on her path unturned. Quan Lee is a courageous woman. She is one of my *sheroes*."
—Carolyn Holbrook, Adjunct Assistant Professor, Dept. of English, Founder
and past Artistic/Executive Director of SASE: The Write Place

"In *Chinese Blackbird*, Sherry Quan Lee renders stories of her complex cultural heritage with the lyrical touch of a poet coming into self-possession. Through the generative power of language, Lee creates an inspirational and a multifarious self. This self blows breath unto the page and into the reader, who may have felt quiescent or invisible, often feeling forced to choose among various enriching worlds, until she experiences the truth that only good literature can unveil about the joys and struggles of defining oneself on one's terms."
—Pamela R. Fletcher, Associate Professor of English Co-Director of Critical
Studies in Race and Ethnicity, College of St. Catherine

www.ModernHistoryPress.com

How to Write a Suicide Note by Sherry Quan Lee

How to Write a Suicide Note examines the life of a Chinese/Black woman who grew up passing for white, who grew up poor, who loves women but has always married white men. Writing has saved her life. It has allowed her to name the historical trauma—the racist, sexist, classist experiences that have kept her from being fully alive, that have screamed at her loudly and consistently that she was no good, and would never be any good-and that no one could love her. Writing has given her the creative power to name the experiences that dictated who she was, even before she was born, and write notes to them, suicide notes.

Sherry Quan Lee believes writing saves lives; writing has saved her life.

"*How to Write a Suicide Note is* a haunting portrait of the daughter of an African mother and a Chinese father. Sherry dares to be who she isn't supposed to be, feel what she isn't supposed to feel, and destroys racial and gender myths as she integrates her bi-racial identity into all that she is. Through her raw honesty and vulnerability, Sherry captures a range of emotions most people are afraid to confront, or even share. Her work is a gift to the mental health community."

—Beth Kyong Lo, M.A., Psychotherapist

"Sherry Quan Lee offers us, in How to Write a Suicide Note, a deep breathing meditation on how love is under continuous revision. And like all the best Blues singers, Quan Lee voices the lowdown, dirty paces that living puts us through, but without regret or surrender"

—Wesley Brown, author *of Darktown Strutters* and *Tragic Magic*

www.ModernHistoryPress.com